The Perfect Book of DOLL CLOTHES

The Perfect Book of DOLL CLOTHES

The Vanessa-Ann Collection

Sterling Publishing Co., Inc. New York

Acknowledgements: The Ceramic masks (page 118) and Paperform (page 74) and porcelain dolls (pages 100, 116, 118, and 122), were provided by Chapelle, Ltd., P.O. Box 9252, Newgate Station, Ogden, Utah 84401.

Library of Congress Cataloging-in-Publication Data

The Perfect book of doll clothes / the Vanessa-Ann Collection.
     p.   cm.
    Includes index.
    ISBN 0-8069-8474-0
    1. Doll clothes—Patterns.   I. Vanessa-Ann Collection (Firm)
TT175.7.P47   1991
745.592'21—dc20   91–22513
                                       CIP

10 9 8 7 6 5 4 3 2 1

Published by Sterling Publishing Company, Inc.
387 Park Avenue South, New York, N.Y. 10016
© 1991 by Chapelle, Ltd.
Distributed in Canada by Sterling Publishing
% Canadian Manda Group, P.O. Box 920, Station U
Toronto, Ontario, Canada M8Z 5P9
Distributed in Great Britain and Europe by Cassell PLC
Villiers House, 41/47 Strand, London WC2N 5JE, England
Distributed in Australia by Capricorn Ltd.
P.O. Box 665, Lane Cove, NSW 2066
Printed in Hong Kong
All rights reserved

Sterling   ISBN 0-8069-8474-0

The Vanessa-Ann Collection

Designers

Terrece Beesley
Trice Boerens
Jo Packham
Florence Stacey

Owners

Terrece Beesley
and Jo Packham

Staff

Ana Ayala
Tricia Barney
Vicki Burke
Gloria Baur
Sandra D. Chapman
Linda Durbano
Tim Fairholm
Susan Jorgensen
Margaret Shields Marti
Barbara Milburn
Lisa Miles
Reva Smith Petersen
Pamela Randall
Gayle Voss
Nancy Whitley

Illustrator

Linda Durbano

Photographer

Ryne Hazen

Contents

Chapter One
SLEEPY TIME
TO
TWINKLING TIME

Baby's sleeping
    On pillows of lace,
And woodland cherubs,
    Dance all over the place.
This happens all the time
    In Chapter One,
Because each and every project
    Is just so much fun.
Confetti Clown is sure
    To make you smile,
And our jester will keep you laughing
    For a long, long while.
Tiptoe through the park
    And let those twinkling stars shine,
This entire chapter will prove
    Absolutely just divine!

Baby Doll

Lullabies and Lace

cut two sleeves (page 23).

MATERIALS

★ 5 yards of 7"-wide nylon flat lace trim with one straight edge
★ 10" of ⅛"-wide elastic
★ ⅝ yard of ⅛"-wide light pink satin ribbon
★ ¾ yard of ¹⁄₁₆"-wide elastic
★ Closures
★ Matching thread

DIRECTIONS

DRESS

1. From lace cut one 40"-long skirt. From straight edge of lace, cut two bodice fronts and four bodice backs. With wrist of sleeve pattern on decorative edge, cut two sleeves (page 23). Cut one 1¼" x 18" ruffle along decorative edge.

2. With decorative edge parallel to waist, position lace over bodice front and bodice backs to cover top two thirds of each. Using bodice patterns as guide, cut one bodice front and two bodices backs. Pin to one bodice front and two bodice backs to make decorative bodice pieces. Proceed to handle all layers of fabric as one.

3. Stitch decorative bodice front and decorative bodice backs together at shoulders. Repeat for remaining bodice pieces. Stitch gathering threads in straight edge of ruffle. Gather to fit neckline. Stitch to right side of decorative bodice neckline with raw edges matching.

4. Place right sides of two bodices together, matching shoulder seams. Stitch along one center back, around neck on stitching line of ruffle, and along second center back. Clip curved seam allowances of neck. Turn. Proceed to handle all layers of fabric as one.

5. Cut elastic into one 9" piece and four 4½" pieces. Stitch one 4½" piece to sleeve ¾" above decorative edge. Stitch gathering threads along sleeve cap; gather to fit armhole. Stitch sleeve cap to bodice. Stitch side seam from bottom of bodice to wrist edge of sleeve, adjusting elastic to fit doll and securing it in seam. Repeat.

6. Fold skirt with right sides together and short ends matching. Stitch short ends to within 2" of top edge; backstitch. (This seam is the center back; the long edge with the opening is the waist.) Fold edges of opening double to wrong side and stitch with a narrow hem.

7. Stitch gathering threads along waist of skirt. Match center fronts and gather skirt to fit bodice; stitch. Attach closures.

BONNET

8. Cut one 27"-long bonnet from lace. Stitch gathering threads 1½" from decorative edge and ½" from straight edge. Tightly gather straight edge. Stitch short ends together, beginning at straight gathered edge and sewing for 2½" only; backstitch. Fold edges of opening double to wrong side and stitch. Stitch over gathering threads to secure the gathers.

9. Place bonnet on doll head. Gather decorative edge of lace to fit doll face; secure threads. Stitch over gathering threads to secure the gathers.

Before cutting any fabric, read the General Instructions, page 138.

10. Cut ribbon into two equal pieces. Fold each in half. Tack fold to front corners of bonnet.

PANTIES

11. Cut two panties from lace with bottom of legs aligned with decorative edge.

12. Stitch center front and center back seams. Fold, aligning center seams.

Stitch one piece of elastic ¾" above decorative edge. Stitch inseam, adjusting elastic to fit doll and securing it in seam.

13. Make ¼"-deep casing on waist edge. Cut one 8½" x 9" piece of elastic. Insert in casing; secure ends. Stitch opening closed.

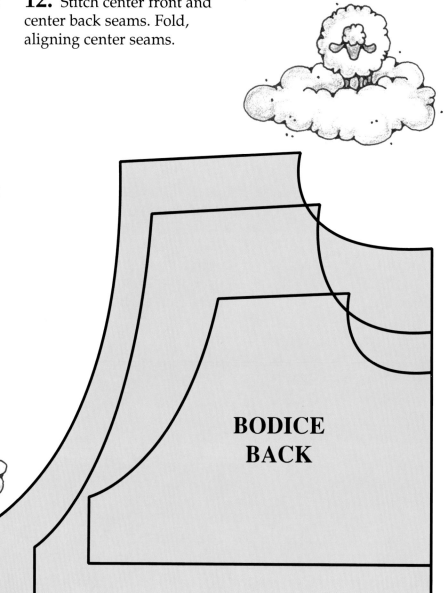

BODICE
BACK

BOOTIES

MATERIALS & TOOLS
★ DMC Pearl Cotton #5, (10 gr. skeins), 1 ball Blanc
★ Size 2 steel hook

GAUGE
Sole size: Approximately 1½" wide x 3½" long.
Sole: Approximately 8 hdc = 1"; 2 hdc and 1 dc row = 1"

All patterns include ¼" seam allowances.

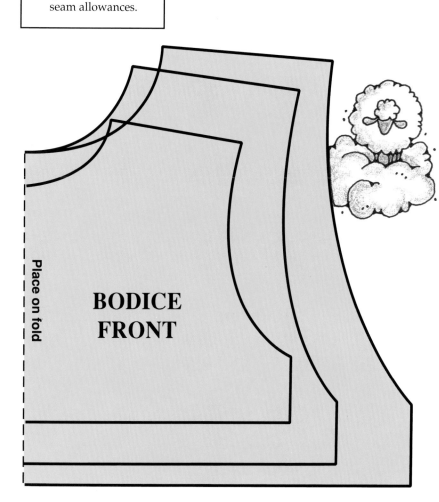

BODICE FRONT

Place on fold

DIRECTIONS
Ch 23.

Rnd 1 (right side): 2 dc in 4th ch from hook for heel, dc in ea of next 17 chs, 7 dc in last ch for toe, turn and work down opposite side of base ch, tr in each of next 17 chs, sl st to top of beg ch.

Rnd 2: Ch 2, hdc in ea st around, sl st to top of beg ch.

Rnd 3: Working behind Rnd 2 and working in sts that Rnd 2 was worked in, sl st in next st, ch 5 (counts as tr and ch 1), [sk next st, tr in next st (to the left of the Rnd 2 sc), ch 1] around, end with sl st to in 4th ch of beg ch-5 = 30 ch-1 sps.

Rnd 4: Sl st in next ch-1, ch 5 (counts as tr and ch 1), (tr in next ch-1, ch 1) around, end with sl st in 4th ch of beg ch-5.

Rnd 5: Sl st into ch-1 sp, 2 hdc in same sp, (2 hdc in next ch-1 sp) 8 times, hdc in each of next 15 ch-1 sps, (2 hdc in next ch-1 sp) 6 times, do not join but continue working in a spiral - mark next st with a safety pin and move it up at end of each rnd.

Rnd 6: Hdc in each of next 24 sts, * dec over next 2 sts as follows: (insert hook in next st, pull up a lp) twice, yo and pull through all lps on hook; rep from * once, hdc in each of next 17 sts.

Rnd 7: Sc in each of next 23 sts, dec over next 2 sts, sc in each of next 18 sts, sl st in next st. Fasten off.

Ankle: Row 1 (wrong side facing): Join thread in 7th st from dec of last rnd, ch 5, sk 1 st, tr in next st, (ch 1, sk 1 st, tr in next st) 13 times, turn.

Row 2: Sl st in 4th ch from hook for picot, [tr in first ch-1 sp, ch 3, sl st in top

of tr for picot] twice, ch 1, *
(tr picot) 3 times in next ch-
1 sp, ch 1; rep from * 12
times more. Fasten off.

RIBBON
To weave ribbon, begin
at center back and work as
shown (Diagram 1).

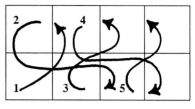

Diagram 1

Before cutting any fabric, read the
General Instructions, page 138.

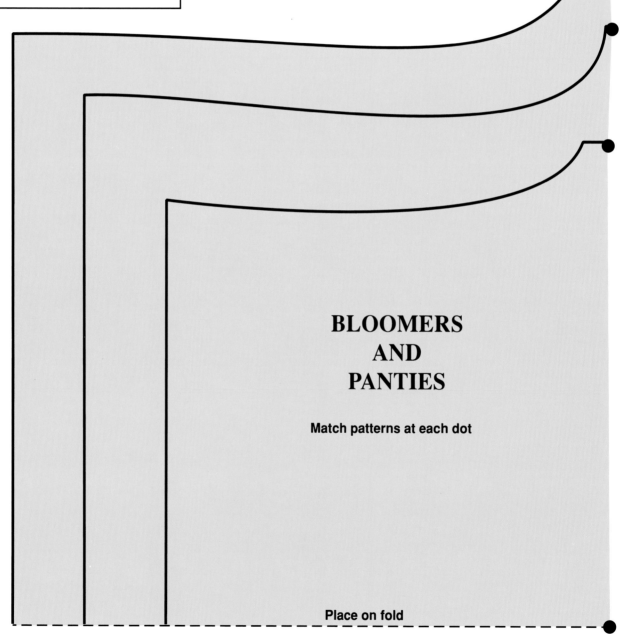

BLOOMERS
AND
PANTIES

Match patterns at each dot

Place on fold

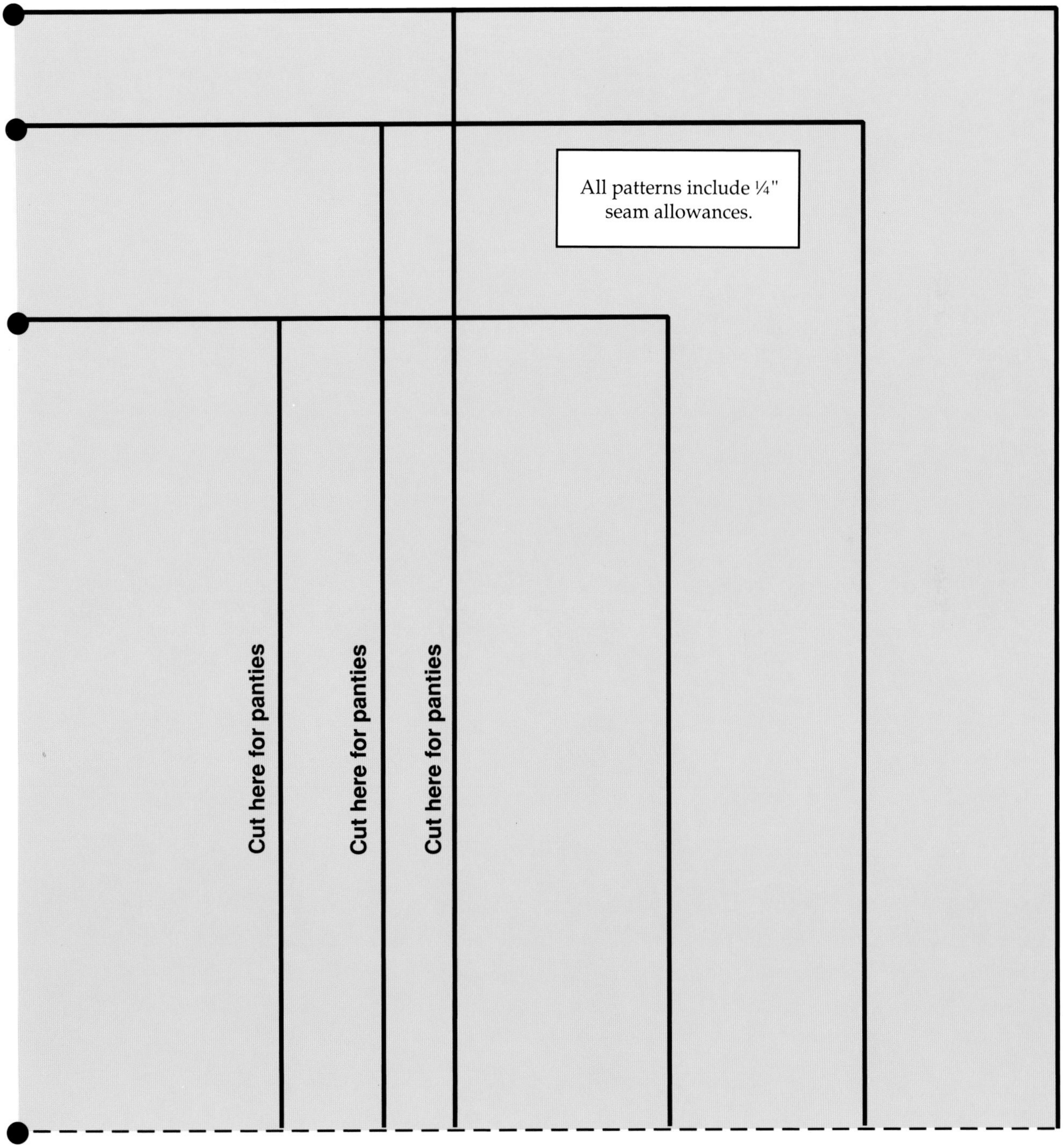

All patterns include ¼" seam allowances.

Cut here for panties

Cut here for panties

Cut here for panties

Baby Doll

Cherished Christening Gown

FABRICS

★ ¾ yard of blue tricot:
Two bodice fronts*
Four bodice backs*
Two sleeves*
One 24" x 9" skirt
One 4" x 96" ruffle
One 4½" x 9" bonnet

★ ½ yard of sheer white tricot:
Two bodice fronts*
Four bodice backs*
Two sleeve caps; see pattern*
One 20" x 48" skirt
One 1" x 8" neck binding

★ Scrap of white satin:
One bonnet back
One 4½" x 9" bonnet
One 1¼" x 10" bonnet binding

MATERIALS

★ Flat white lace with one straight edge as follows:
7 yards of 6"-wide lace
3 yards of 4"-wide lace
1½ yards of 1"-wide lace

★ 2¼ yards of 2"-wide flat white trim

★ 3 yards of ⅜"-wide white satin ribbon

★ 1 yard of ¼"-wide white satin ribbon

★ ½ yard of ⅛"-wide elastic

★ Closures

★ Matching threads

★ Dressmakers' pen

* Patterns on pages 10, 11 and 23.

center back. Clip curved seam allowances of neck. Turn. Proceed to handle both layers of fabric as one.

2. Stitch a narrow hem in wrist edge of one sleeve. Cut elastic into four equal pieces. Stitch one piece of elastic ¾" above hem. Stitch gathering threads along sleeve cap; gather to fit armhole. Stitch sleeve cap to bodice. Repeat.

3. Stitch side seam from bottom of bodice to hem of sleeve, adjusting elastic to fit doll and securing it in seam. Repeat.

DIRECTIONS

BLUE UNDERDRESS

1. Stitch one blue bodice front to two blue bodice backs at shoulders. Repeat with remaining bodice front and bodice backs. Place right sides of two bodices together, matching shoulder seams. Stitch along one center back seam, around neck and along second

4. Stitch narrow hem in one long edge of ruffle. Stitch gathering threads along second long edge. Match center fronts and gather ruffle to fit one long edge of skirt; stitch.

5. Fold skirt/ruffle with right sides together and short ends matching. Stitch short ends to within 3" of long raw edge; backstitch. (This seam is the center back; the long edge with the opening is the waist.) Fold edges of opening double to wrong side and stitch with narrow hem.

6. Stitch gathering threads along waist edge of skirt. Match center fronts and gather skirt to fit bodice; stitch Zigzag over raw edges of seam allowance at waistline. Attach closures.

WHITE OVERDRESS

7. Complete Step 1 using white tricot. Cut one 16" piece of 1"-wide lace. Stitch gathering threads along straight edge. Match center fronts of neck and wrong side of lace. Gather lace to fit neck and topstitch. Stitch one long edge of neck binding to neck/lace. Fold double to inside and slipstitch, then fold sides under and slipstitch.

8. Cut one 18" piece of 6"-wide lace. Stitch gathering threads along straight edge. Match centers and gather lace to fit straight edge of sleeve; topstitch, placing seam ¼" below straight edge of lace.

9. Cut one 4" piece of elastic. Stitch elastic ⅝" above wrist edge of sleeve. Stitch gathering threads along sleeve cap; gather to fit armhole. Stitch sleeve cap to bodice. Repeat.

10. From 2"-wide trim, cut one piece 7" long, and depending upon pattern of trim, about 1"-wide. Also cut one 7" piece of ⅜"-wide ribbon. Place decorative edge of trim up bodice front, over shoulders and down bodice back, parallel to and overlapping sleeve seam ¼"; baste. Place ribbon over opposite edge of trim. Topstitch both edges of ribbon, securing trim. Repeat on opposite side of bodice. Complete Step 3 for blue underdress.

11. Cut two 90" pieces of 6"-wide lace. Stitch gathering threads along straight edge of both pieces. Match center fronts and gather one piece of lace to fit one long edge of topstitch, placing seam ¼" below straight edge of lace.

12. Mark parallel lines 3½", 7½" and 11½" above lace. Place straight edge of second piece of lace on 3½" line. Match center fronts and gather lace to fit skirt; stitch, placing seam ¼" below straight edge of lace.

13. Cut one 48" piece of 2"-wide trim. Cut one 48" piece of ⅜"-wide ribbon. Baste lace to skirt on 7½" line. Place ribbon over straight edge of lace; topstitch both edges, securing trim.

14. On 11½" line, mark 2½" from each side of center front. Mark ½" below center front of waist. Beginning at this mark, make a line that

curves to meet each side mark. Stitch gathering threads on straight edge of 4"-wide lace. Match mark at center front of waist with center front of lace and gather lace to fit curved line and 11½" line; topstitch, placing seam ¼" below straight edge of lace.

15. Fold skirt/ruffles with right sides together and short ends matching. Stitch to within 3" of raw edge; backstitch. (This seam is the center back; the long edge with the opening is the waist.) Fold the edges of opening double to wrong side and stitch with a narrow hem.

16. Stitch gathering threads along waist of skirt. Match center fronts and gather skirt to fit bodice; stitch. Zigzag over raw edges of seam allowances.

17. From 2"-wide trim, cut one piece 14" long and, depending upon pattern of trim, about 1" wide. Also cut one 14" piece of ⅜"-wide ribbon. Place straight edge of trim over waist seam. Place ribbon over straight edge of trim. Topstitch both edges of ribbon, securing the trim.

18. Tie ¼"-wide ribbon into bow. Tack to the center front of the dress. Attach the closures.

BONNET

19. With right sides of 4½" x 9" satin and tricot pieces together, stitch one long edge; turn. Cut 1 yard of 6"-wide lace. Stitch gathering threads along straight edge of lace and 1" from decorative edge. Gather both edges to 9". Place lace over tricot; baste. Stitch gathering threads along straight edge of satin/ tricot/lace. Match center front with center top of bonnet back. Gather to fit bonnet back; stitch, securing all layers.

20. Stitch one long edge of bonnet binding to lower edge of bonnet. Fold double to inside and slipstitch, securing all layers. Cut two 18" pieces of ⅜"-wide ribbon. Make two ½" deep folds in one end of each piece. Tack folds to front corners of bonnet.

Before cutting any fabric, read the General Instructions, page 138.

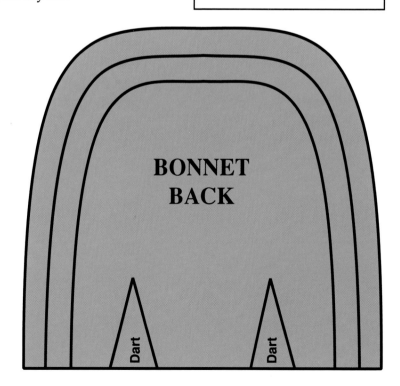

BONNET BACK

Dart   Dart

Baby Doll

Confetti Clown

FABRICS

- ★ 1½ yards white sparkle:
  One top front
  Two top backs
  Two sleeves
  Two bloomers*
  One hat
  One 8" x 36" ruffle
  Two 6" x 18" wrist
    ruffles
  Two 6" x 18" ankle
    ruffles
  One 3" x 17" hat band
  One 3" x 22" top band
  Two 1" x 17" bias strips
    for shoes

- ★ ¾ yard white:
  One top front
  Two top backs
  Two bloomers*
  Two sleeves
- ★ ¾ yard blue shiny satin:
  One hat
  One 3" x 17" hat band
  One 8" x 36" ruffle
  Two shoe soles
  Two shoe tongues
  Two 3" x 6" shoe sides
- ★ ¼ yard blue, pink and
  yellow tricot:
  ½"-wide strips of
    assorted lengths
*Pattern on page 12

MATERIALS

- ★ ¼ yard of blue picot
  ribbon
- ★ One skein of lavender
  100% cotton
  mercerized yarn
- ★ 1 yard of ¹⁄₁₆"-wide blue
  satin ribbon
- ★ 1 yard of ¼"-wide blue
  picot ribbon
- ★ One 4" x 10" piece of
  cardboard

- ★ 1 yard of ¼"-wide
  elastic
- ★ Two small white yarn
  pom-poms
- ★ One small blue yarn
  pom-pom
- ★ One large white yarn
  pom-pom
- ★ Closures
- ★ Matching threads

DIRECTIONS

1. Stitch sparkle top front and two sparkle top backs together at shoulders. Stitch center back to within 5" of neck. Repeat with white top and backs. Place right sides of two tops together, matching shoulder seams. Stitch neck and center back opening. Clip curved seam allowance. Turn.

2. Stitch side seams in sparkle fabric. Then stitch side seams in white fabric.

3. Place nine to ten long tricot strips on shoulder seam between layers of top, altering lengths. Stitch through all strips in shoulder seam. Repeat.

4. Fold one wrist ruffle in half, matching long edges. Stitch gathering threads on long edges. Gather to fit wrist of sleeve. Pin one white and one sparkle sleeve together. Stitch ruffle to wrist edge, using a ½" seam. Fold all raw edges to wrong side of white sleeve. Stitch ⅜" from and parallel to seam, making a casing. Place tricot strips between sparkle and white fabrics at sleeve cap; baste. With edges of all layers together, stitch gathering threads in sleeve cap. Cut one 5" piece of elastic. Thread elastic through casing; secure ends. With right sides of sparkle fabric together, stitch sleeve/ruffle seam, adjusting elastic to fit doll and securing it in seam. Gather sleeve cap to fit armhole; set in sleeve. Repeat.

5. Working with top upside down, place tricot strips between layers of top. Match bottom edges of top. Stitch gathering threads through both layers. Fold top band in half, matching short edges; stitch. Turn. Fold top band again with wrong sides together and matching long edges. Gather top to fit top band; stitch. Attach closures. Space evenly and tack pompoms to center front of top.

BLOOMERS

6. Match one sparkle bloomers to one white bloomers and proceed to handle both layers of fabric as one. Fold one ankle ruffle in half, matching long edges. Stitch gathering threads on long edge. Gather to fit ankle of bloomers. Stitch ruffle to ankle edge, using a ½" seam. Fold all raw edges to wrong side of white bloomers. Stitch ⅜" from and parallel to ruffle seam, making a casing. Cut one 6" piece of elastic. Thread elastic through casing; secure ends. With right sides of sparkle fabric together, stitch inseam/ruffle, adjusting elastic to fit doll and securing it in seam. Repeat to make other leg. Place one leg inside the other with right sides together. Stitch center seam.

Turn. Make ½" casing at waist. Cut one 17" piece of elastic. Insert elastic in casing; secure. Slipstitch casing closed.

HAT

7. Stitch long edges of sparkle hat together. Repeat with blue hat. Place right side of blue hat inside and next to wrong side of sparkle hat. Place tricot strips between layers. Match bottom edges of hat. Stitch gathering threads through both layers. Fold hat band in half, matching short edges; stitch. Turn. Fold hat band again, matching long edges. Gather hat to fit hat band. Stitch hat band to bottom edge of hat. Tack large pom pom to point of hat.

8. To attach hair to hat, wrap yarn around 4" ends of cardboard. Cut a small amount of yarn at fold on one edge of cardboard. Place the remaining fold over seam which joins the band to the hat; stitch yarn to hat. Repeat to fill whole distance around hat band.

RUFFLE

9. Place sparkle and blue ruffles together. Stitch all edges, leaving an opening. Clip corners. Turn. Slipstitch opening closed. Mark 3¼" from one long edge of blue fabric. Place 1/16"-wide ribbon lengthwise on ruffle at mark and zigzag in large loose stitches over ribbon. Gather ruffle and ribbon.

SHOES

10. Stitch sparkle bias to tongue; see pattern. Stitch sparkle bias to ends and one long edge of side piece. Stitch 2" piece of elastic 1¾" below bias edge of side; secure ends ¼" from ends of side. Match centers of heel and side piece; stitch. Then match centers of tongue and sole; see * on pattern. Stitch, overlapping the tongue and side. Turn. Cut four 9" pieces of picot ribbon. Attach one to each end of the side piece on right side of fabric where the elastic ends. Repeat.

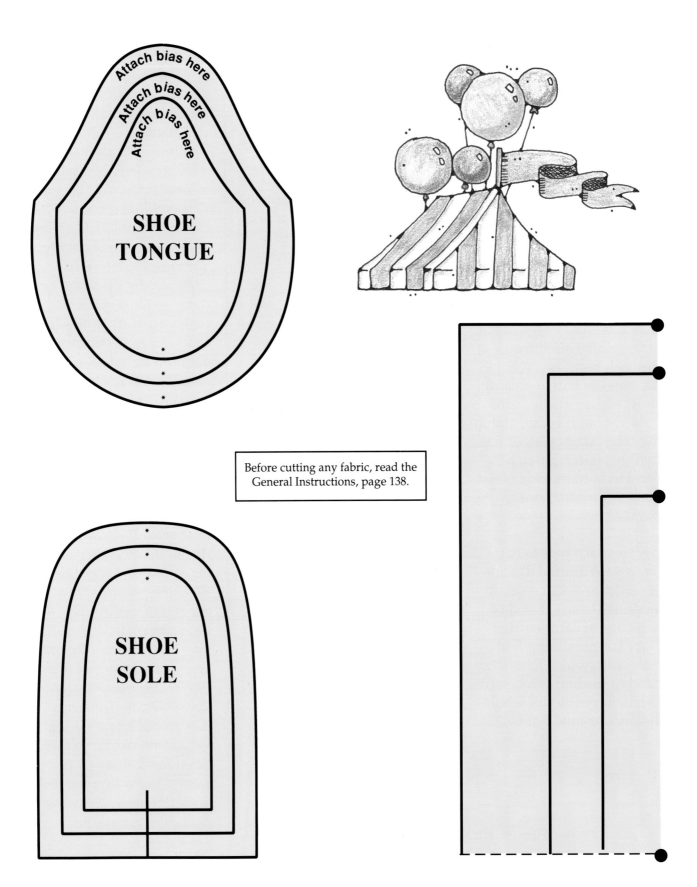

SHOE TONGUE

Attach bias here
Attach bias here
Attach bias here

*
*
*

SHOE SOLE

*
*
*

Before cutting any fabric, read the General Instructions, page 138.

All patterns include ¼"
seam allowances.

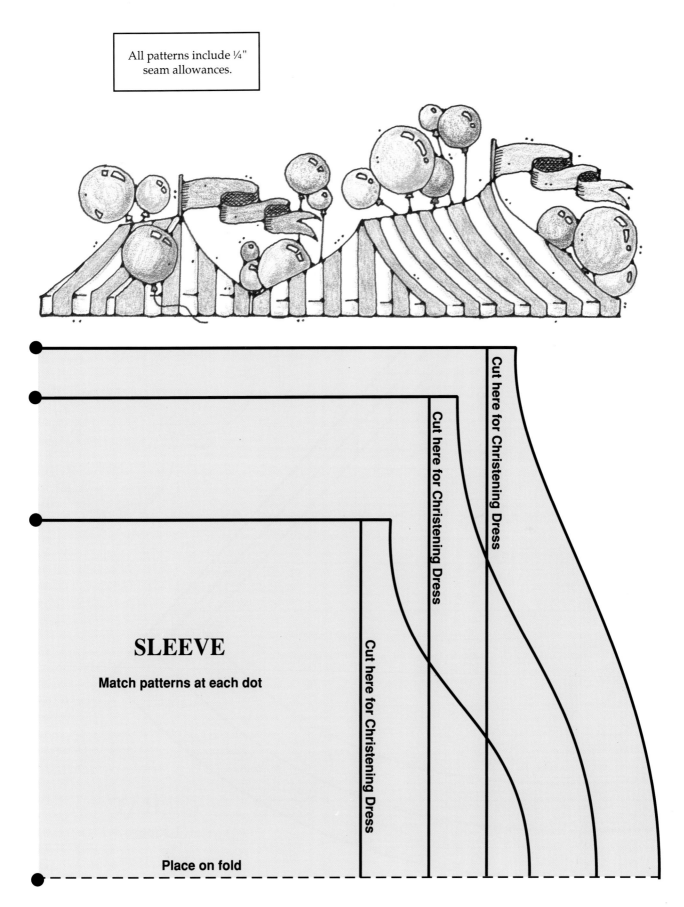

Cut here for Christening Dress

Cut here for Christening Dress

SLEEVE

Match patterns at each dot

Cut here for Christening Dress

Place on fold

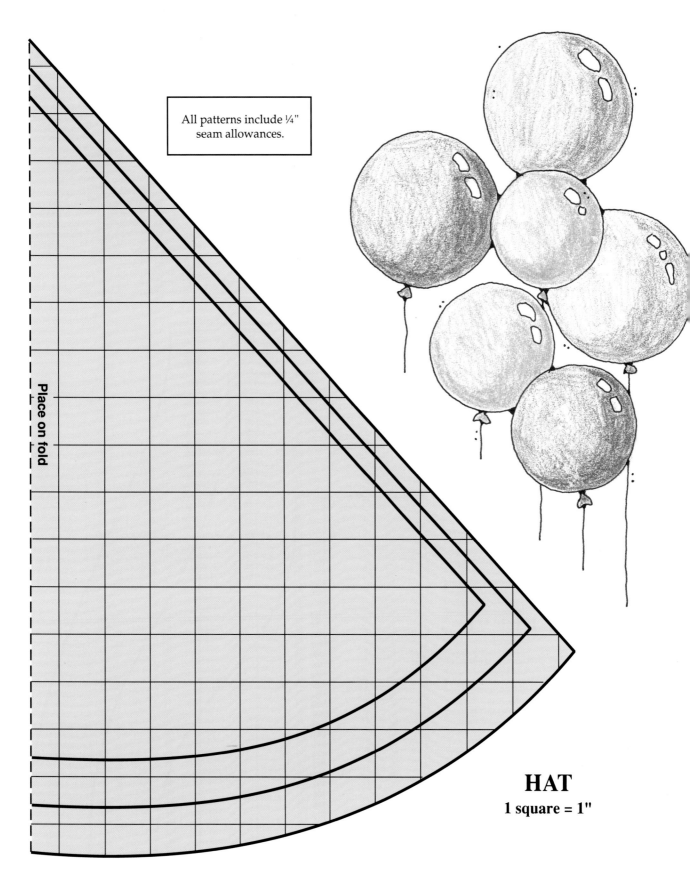

All patterns include ¼"
seam allowances.

Place on fold

HAT

1 square = 1"

TOP
FRONT
AND
BACK

1 square = 1"

All patterns include ¼"
seam allowances.

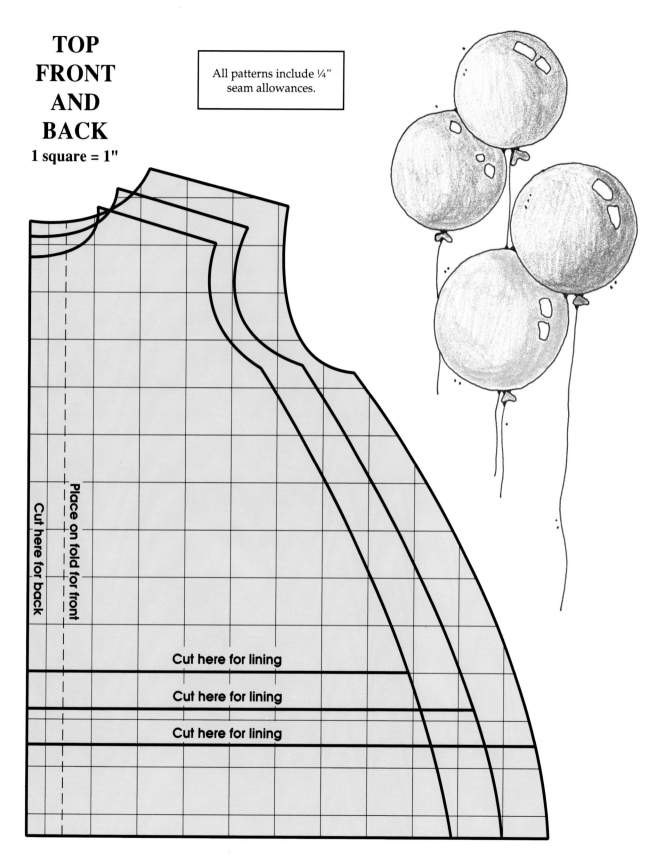

Cut here for back

Place on fold for front

Cut here for lining

Cut here for lining

Cut here for lining

Baby Doll

Jests & Jingles

FABRICS

★ ⅝ yard of burgundy
satin:
Two jumpsuit fronts
Two jumpsuit backs
Two sleeves
One 4½" x 22" ruffle
One 1½" x 15" bias
casing
★ ¼ yard of tan satin:
One 2½" x 13" belt
One 6" x 22" ruffle
★ ⅜ yard of print satin:
Two collars
Two hats
One 2½" x 13½"
hat band
Four shoes

MATERIALS

★ 2 yards of ¹⁄₁₆"-wide
burgundy ribbon
★ 1" of ¾"-wide hook
and loop tape
★ ½ yard of ⅛"-wide
elastic
★ Stuffing
★ Two large jingle bells
★ One large-eyed needle
★ Three small jingle bells
★ Closures
★ Matching thread

DIRECTIONS

JUMPSUIT

1. Stitch center of two jumpsuit fronts together. Stitch center of two jumpsuit backs together, backstitching on placket. Fold edges of placket double to wrong side; stitch. Stitch jumpsuit front to back at shoulders. Fold casing, matching long edges. Fold ¼" to inside on each end. Stitch casing to neck. Fold all raw edges to inside and topstitch through all layers on jumpsuit. Cut one 27" piece of ribbon; thread through casing.

2. Stitch a narrow hem in wrist edge of one sleeve. Cut elastic into four equal pieces. Stitch one piece of elastic ¾" above hem. Stitch gathering threads along sleeve cap; gather to fit armhole. Stitch sleeve cap to jumpsuit. Repeat.

3. Stitch one side seam from bottom of jumpsuit to hem of sleeve, adjusting elastic to fit doll and securing it in seam. Repeat.

4. Stitch narrow hem in ankle edge of one jumpsuit leg. Stitch one piece of elastic ¾" above hem. Repeat. Stitch inseam, adjusting elastic to fit doll and securing it in seam.

COLLAR

5. Cut from neck down center back of two collars. Stitch outside edges of two collars together. Clip curved seam allowances and corners. Turn. Slipstitch edges of center back opening and neck closed, clipping seam allowances as needed. Attach closures.

RUFFLE

6. Fold tan ruffle in half, matching long edges. Stitch long edge. Turn. Fold each end ¼" to inside. Fold ruffle with seam not quite in center back. Pin. Repeat with burgundy ruffle. Center burgundy ruffle over tan ruffle, without placing all bulk of seam allowances together. Place 24" piece of ribbon lengthwise in center of burgundy ruffle. Zigzag in large loose stitches over ribbon. Gather ruffle to fit doll.

BELT

7. Fold belt in half, matching long edges. Stitch all edges, leaving an opening. Clip corners. Turn. Slipstitch opening closed. Knot center of belt. Stitch hook and loop tape to each end.

SHOES

8. Stitch curved edges of two shoes together. Clip curved seam allowance. Turn. Fold ¼" inside ankle. Cut one 9"-piece of ribbon. Using ribbon, sew running stitches close to ankle edge, beginning and ending at center front. Stuff toe firmly. Repeat. Tack one small jingle bell to toe of each shoe.

HAT

9. Stitch two hats together. Clip curved seam allowances and corners. Turn. Fold hat band in half, matching short edges; stitch. Turn. Fold hat band again, matching long edges. Stitch long edges to right side of bottom edge of hat. Fold to right side of hat. Stuff firmly to within 1" of bottom. Adjust to fit doll. Tack one large jingle bell to each point of hat.

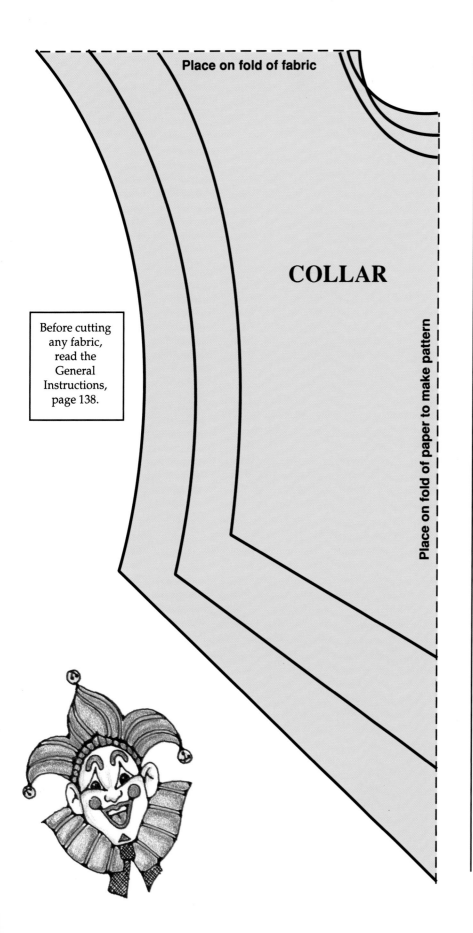

Place on fold of fabric

COLLAR

Place on fold of paper to make pattern

Before cutting any fabric, read the General Instructions, page 138.

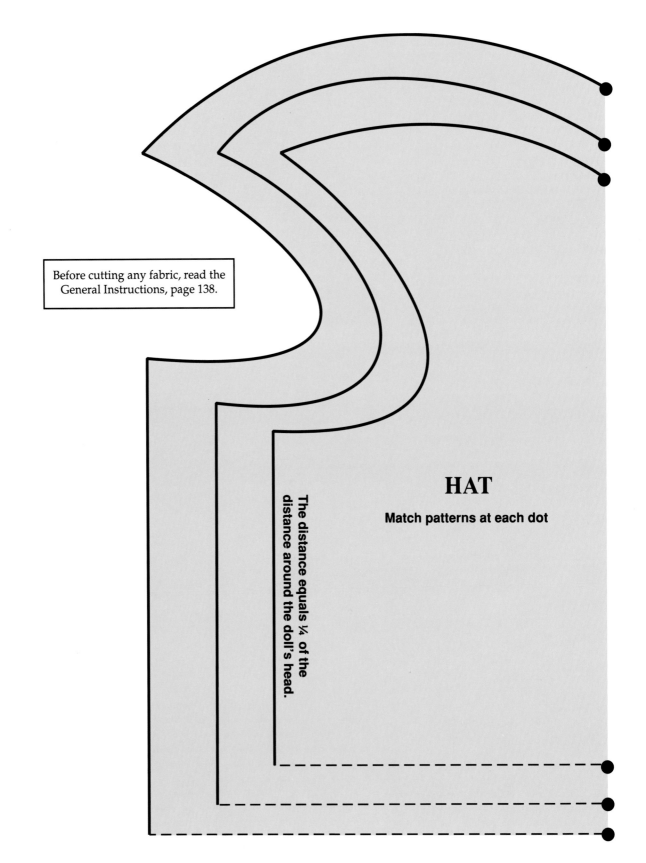

Before cutting any fabric, read the
General Instructions, page 138.

HAT

Match patterns at each dot

The distance equals ¼ of the
distance around the doll's head.

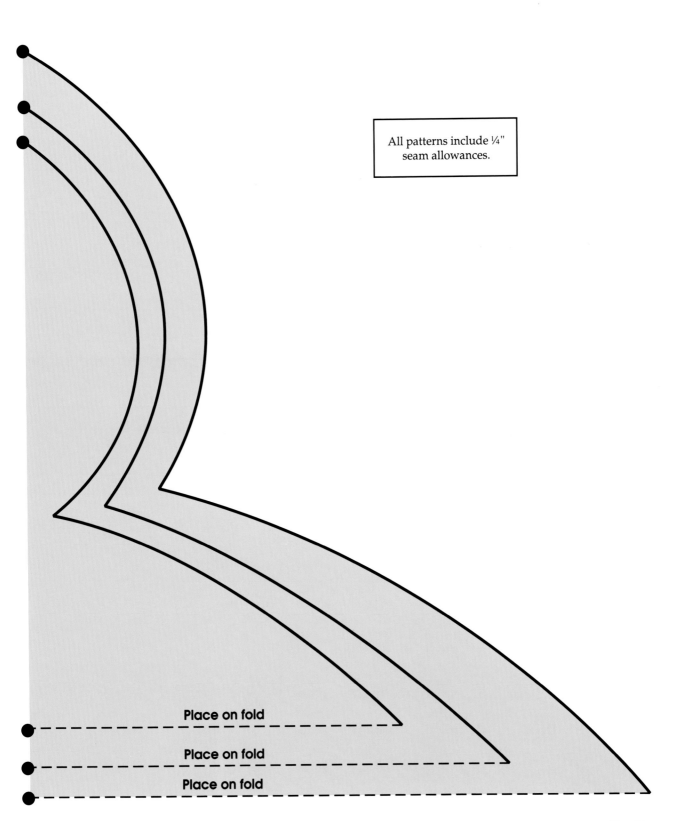

All patterns include ¼"
seam allowances.

Place on fold

Place on fold

Place on fold

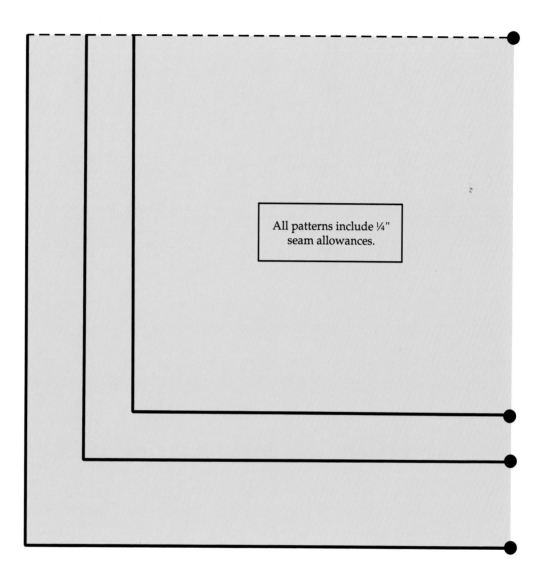

All patterns include ¼"
seam allowances.

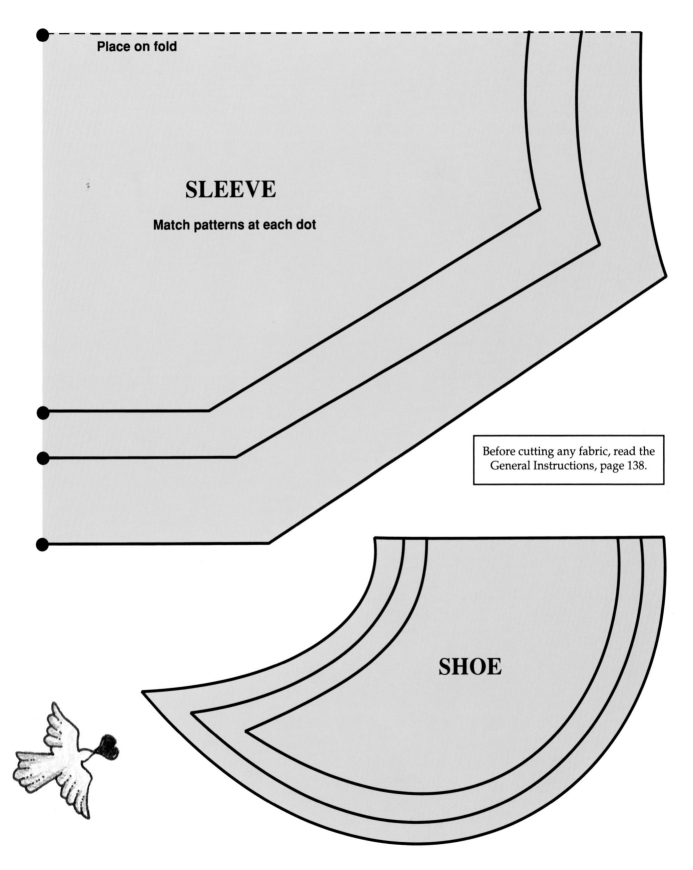

Place on fold

SLEEVE

Match patterns at each dot

Before cutting any fabric, read the
General Instructions, page 138.

SHOE

JUMPSUIT
FRONT AND BACK

1 square = 1"

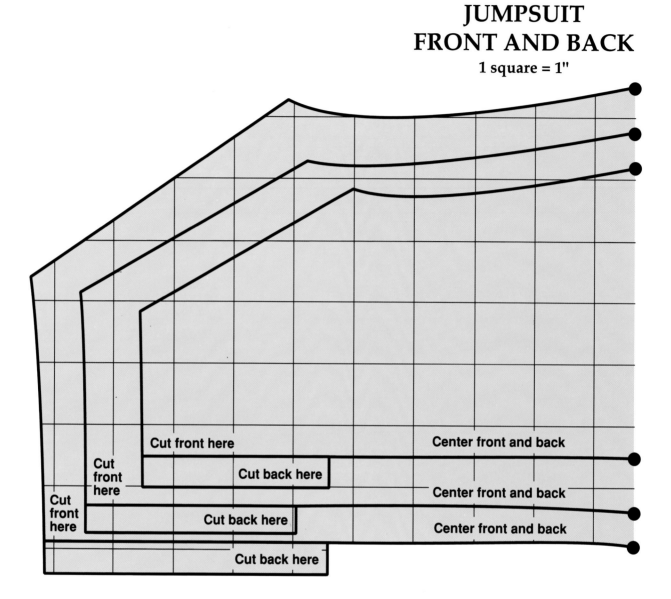

Cut front here

Center front and back

Cut
front
here

Cut back here

Center front and back

Cut
front
here

Cut back here

Center front and back

Cut back here

Match patterns at each dot

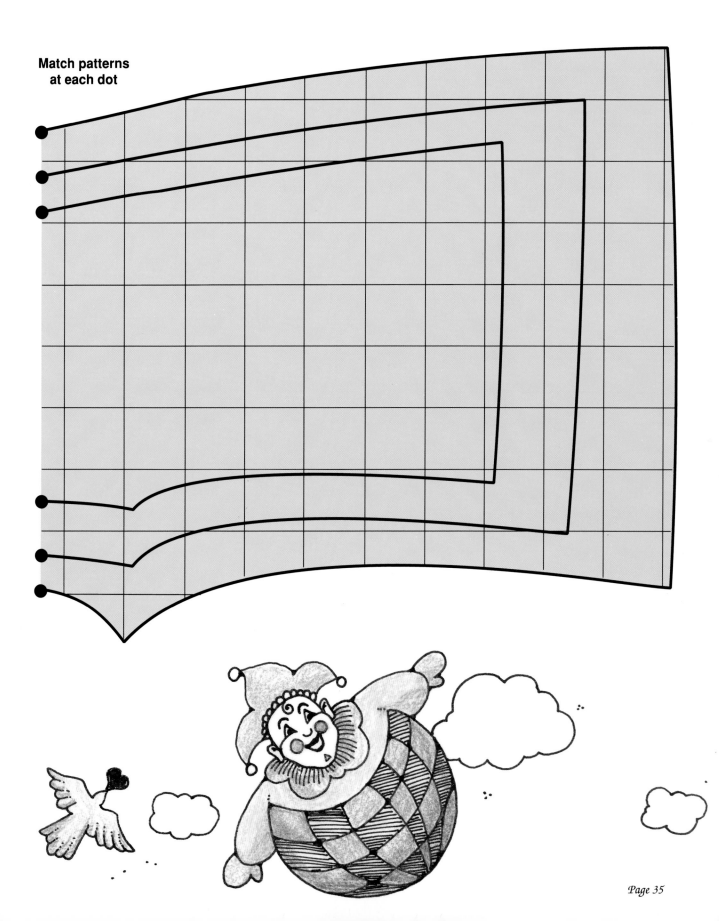

Baby Doll

Woodland Cherub

FABRICS

★ ⅜ yard of green satin:
   Two bodice fronts*
   Four bodice backs*
   Two sleeves*
   54 leaves
   One 1½" x 18" ruffle
   Two shoe sides
   Two shoe soles
★ ¼ yard of apricot crépe:
   Five large petals
★ ⅜ yard of apricot tricot:
   Ten large petals
   Eight medium petals
   Eight small petals

MATERIALS

★ 2½ yards of variegated wired ribbon
★ Peach silk flowers
★ One small spray of peach flowers
★ Two small butterflies
★ Eight plastic leaf beads
★ ½ yard of ⅛"-wide elastic
★ Closures
★ Matching threads

*Patterns on pages 10, 11 and 23.

DIRECTIONS

1. Fold ruffle in half, matching long edges. Stitch ends. Turn. Stitch gathering threads on raw edges.

2. Stitch two leaves together. Clip point. Turn and press. Repeat with all remaining leaves.

3. Stitch one bodice front to one bodice back. Repeat with remaining bodice fronts and backs. Matching center fronts, gather ruffle to fit neck, placing ends of ruffle ¼" from center back

edges. Place right sides of two bodices together, matching shoulder seams. Stitch along one center back seam, around neck, securing ruffle in seam, and along second center back seam. Clip curved seam allowances. Turn. Proceed to handle both layers of fabric as one.

4. Stitch narrow hem in wrist of one sleeve. Cut elastic in half. Stitch one piece of elastic ½" above hem. Stitch gathering threads in sleeve cap. Pin raw edges of five leaves to armhole, placing one on shoulder seam and overlapping others slightly. Gather sleeve to fit armhole. Stitch sleeve cap to bodice, securing leaves in seam. Repeat.

5. Stitch side seam from bottom of bodice to hem of sleeve, adjusting elastic to fit doll and securing it in seam. Repeat.

6. Pin remaining leaves to waist of dress, beginning at center front; baste.

7. Stitch narrow hem in edges of each petal, using nylon fishing line in rolled hem. Feed fishing line through roller hemmer foot inside the hem itself. Use a zigzag stitch to secure (Diagram 1). For best results, place the fishing line above the hemmer foot.

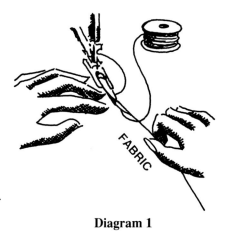

Diagram 1

8. Layer crépe petals side-by-side on flat surface. Then layer tricot petals, overlapping edges and placing smallest at top. Match top edges of all layers. Stitch gathering threads around top edge. Match center fronts and gather to fit bodice; stitch. Attach closures.

9. Cut one 27" piece of ribbon. Tie in bow around waist. Add flowers, five leaf beads and two butterflies. Tack one silk bud and three leaf beads to one shoulder of dress. Cut two 18" pieces of ribbon. Tie in bows around wrists. Cut one 8" piece of ribbon. Wrap around stem of flowers. Cut one 12" piece of ribbon. Tie in bow around bouquet. Glue spray of flowers to doll hand. Twist remaining ribbon tightly and wind through spray. Decorate hair as desired.

SHOES

10. Match center back of shoe side to center back of sole. Stitch along sole to within ¼" of point. Return to center back and stitch opposite side, making stitching meet. Stitch toe of shoe, meeting stitching on sole. Repeat.

11. Fold under ¼" around top edge of shoe. Zigzag elastic to inside edge. Stuff toe firmly. Repeat.

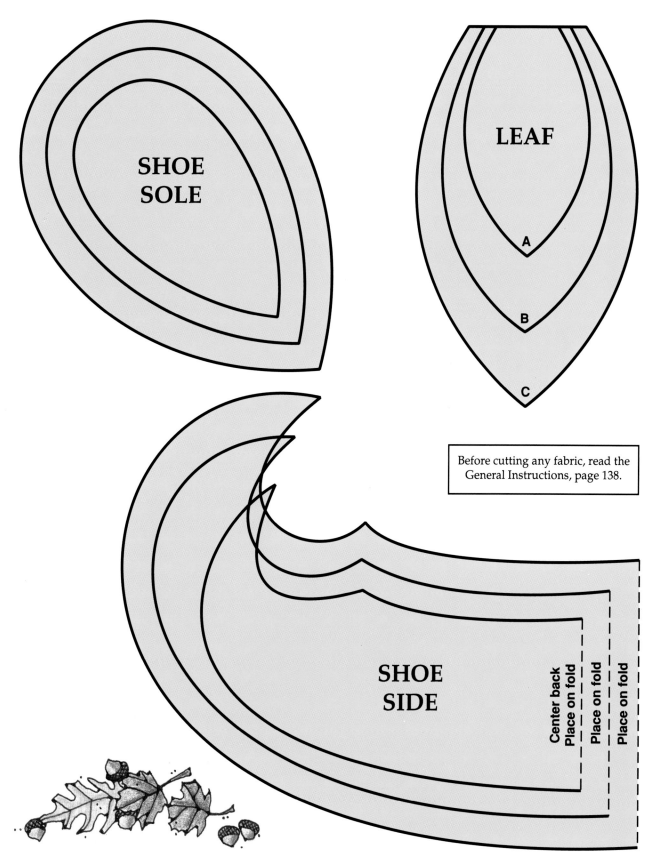

SHOE
SOLE

LEAF

A

B

C

Before cutting any fabric, read the
General Instructions, page 138.

SHOE
SIDE

Center back
Place on fold

Place on fold

Place on fold

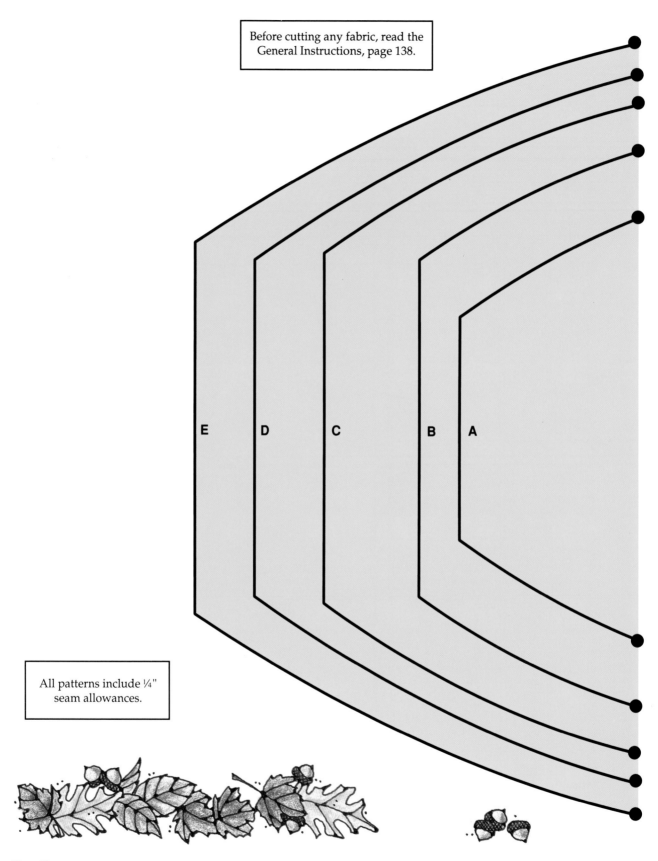

Before cutting any fabric, read the
General Instructions, page 138.

E   D   C   B A

All patterns include ¼"
seam allowances.

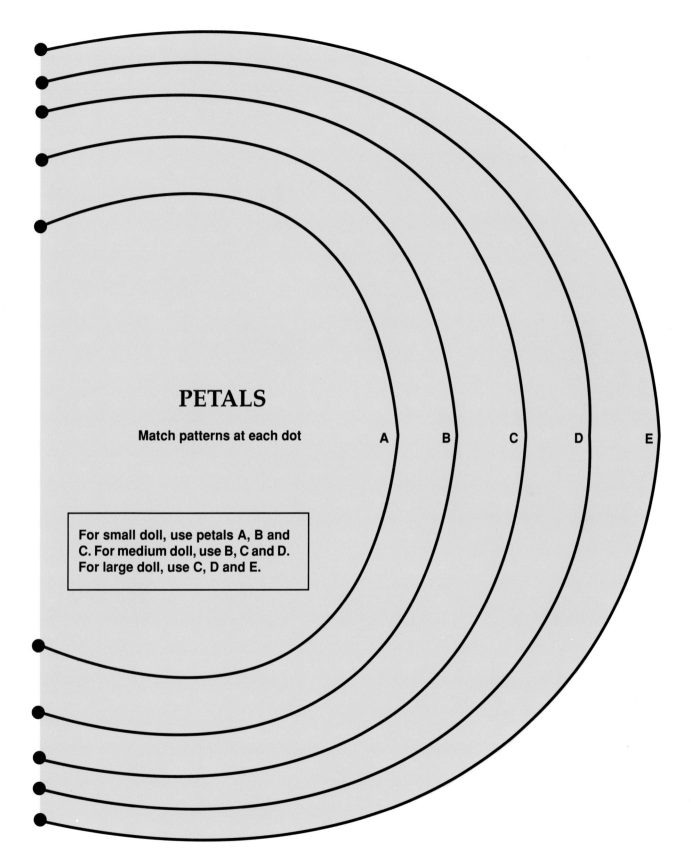

PETALS

Match patterns at each dot

A   B   C   D   E

For small doll, use petals A, B and
C. For medium doll, use B, C and D.
For large doll, use C, D and E.

Barefoot in the Park

FABRICS

★ ½ yard of print:
 Two dress fronts
 Two dress backs
 Two sleeves
 One 2" x 43" ruffle
★ Scrap of solid:
 Four collars
★ Scrap of contrasting
 print:
 One scarf
★ Scrap of contrasting
 solid:
 One 9½" x 1½"
  neck binding
★ Scrap of cotton
 netting:
 One 9½"-wide circle

MATERIALS

★ ⅝ yard of narrow
 trim
★ ¾ yard of 2"-wide
 trim
★ One small purchased
 appliqué
★ Four buttons
★ Closures
★ Matching threads

DIRECTIONS

1. Stitch two dress fronts together at center, then stitch dress front to dress backs at shoulders.

2. Stitch a 1½" hem in wrist edge of one sleeve. Stitch sleeve cap to dress. Repeat. Stitch side seam from bottom of dress to hem of sleeve. Repeat. Stitch narrow hem in long edges of center back.

3. Spread dress out on flat surface. Center and pin netting circle over neck opening. Cut netting to match, then down center back. Pin netting to the neck of dress.

4. Stitch two collars together. Repeat. Pin to neck of dress, meeting at center front. Bind neck edges, securing collar and netting.

5. Make a 1½"-deep tuck 1¼" from bottom of dress.

6. Stitch narrow hem in one long edge of ruffle. Stitch gathering threads in opposite long edge. Match centers of ruffle and bottom edge of dress. Gather ruffle to fit dress; stitch.

7. Sew narrow trim to edge of tuck, covering top edge of ruffle. Attach closures to center back edges. Sew wide trim to bottom edge of dress under ruffle. Evenly space and sew buttons to center front seam. Stitch appliqué to front of dress where desired. Tie scarf around shoulders with knot at center front.

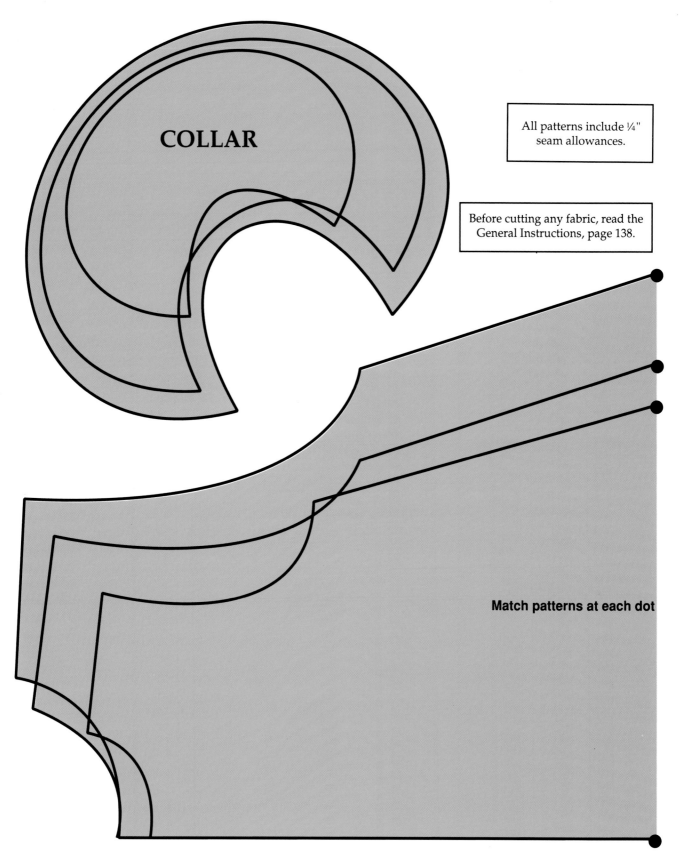

COLLAR

All patterns include ¼"
seam allowances.

Before cutting any fabric, read the
General Instructions, page 138.

Match patterns at each dot

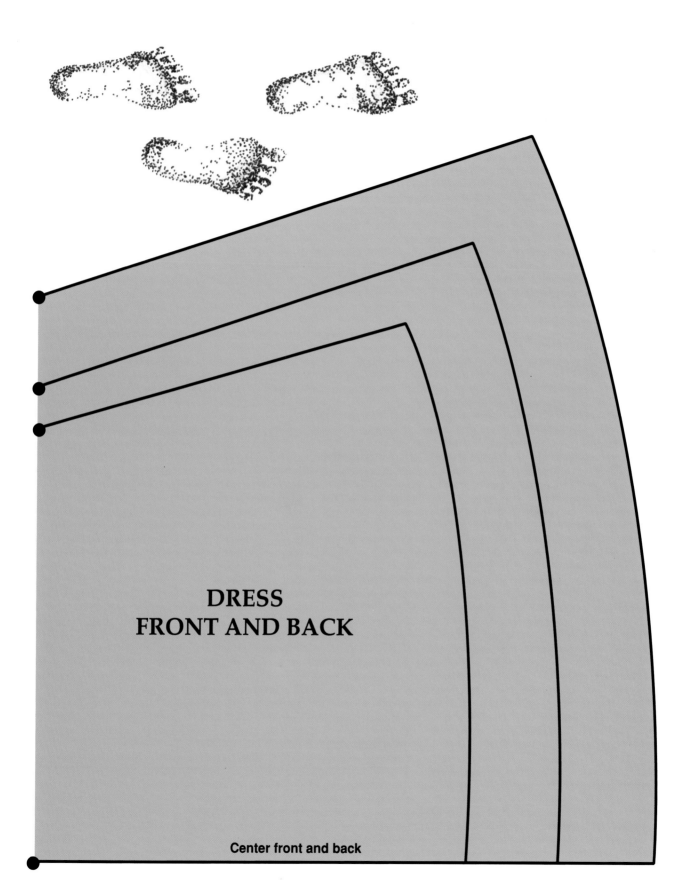

**DRESS
FRONT AND BACK**

Center front and back

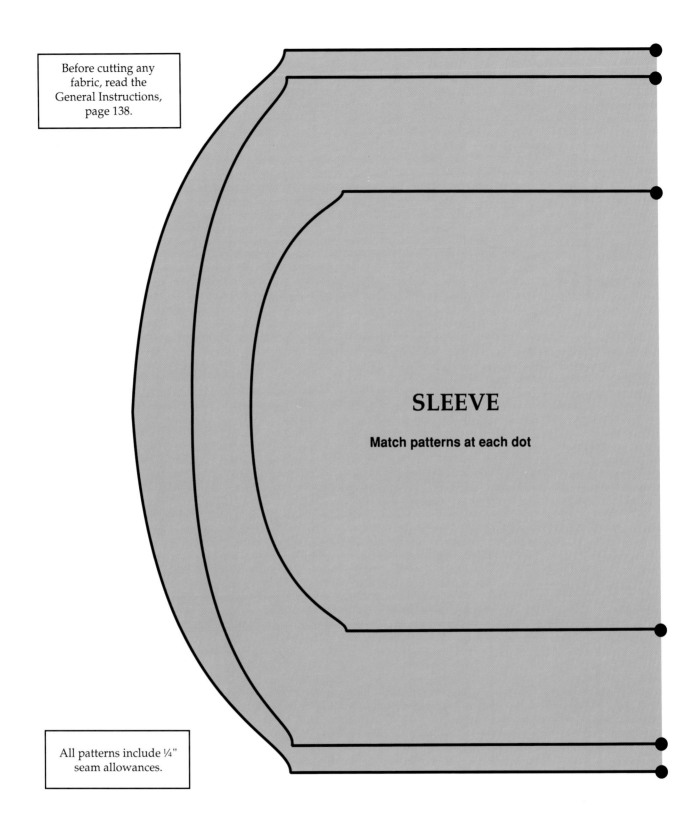

Before cutting any
fabric, read the
General Instructions,
page 138.

SLEEVE

Match patterns at each dot

All patterns include ¼"
seam allowances.

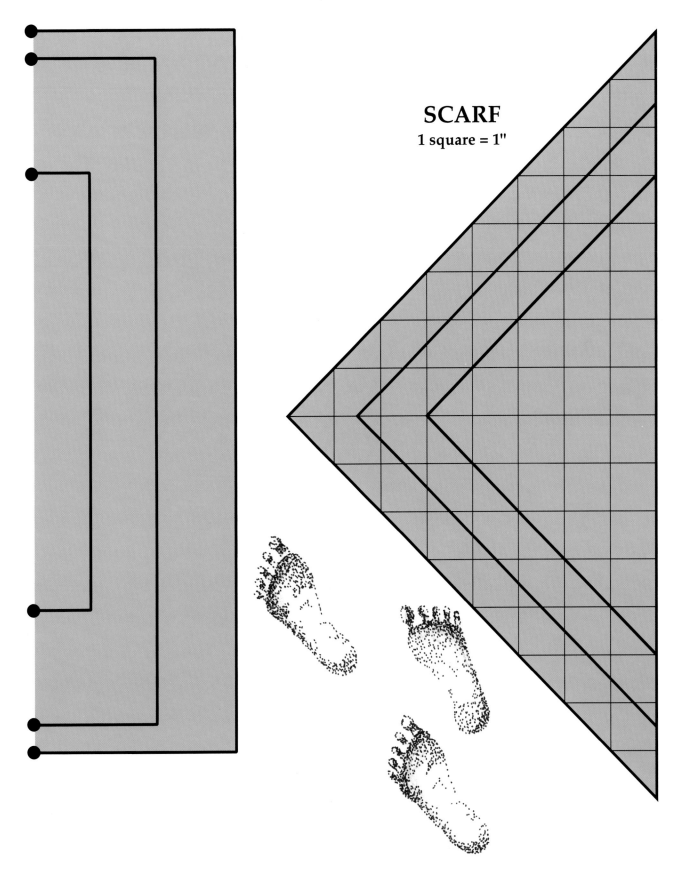

SCARF

1 square = 1"

Baby Doll

Twinkling Stars

MATERIALS for Doll #1	MATERIALS for Doll #2
★ One short sleeve child's T-shirt*	★ Two short sleeve child's T-shirts*
★ 2 yards of ⅛"-wide satin ribbon	★ One 15" x 32" piece cream cotton netting
★ 15" of ⅛"-wide elastic	★ ¼ yard of covered corded piping
★ Blue acrylic paint	★ Acrylic paints: yellow, pink
★ Paint brushes	★ Paint brushes
★ One medium star stencil	★ One large star stencil
★ One small star stencil	★ One small star stencil
★ 8" piece of star tinsel	★ One skein sportweight cotton bouclé yarn
★ Scrap paper	★ One 8" x 36" piece of ¼"-thick foam rubber
★ Safety pins	★ Scrap paper
★ Two closures	★ Two closures
★ Matching threads	★ Matching threads

To select correct T-shirt size, measure doll from one wrist to other across shoulder back. Select a T-shirt 2" to 4" wider from sleeve edge to sleeve edge. The finished outfit is intended to fit loosely.

DIRECTIONS for Doll #1

1. Place shirt on doll. Pin a 1" to 1½"-deep tuck in back of neckline. Measure 4" above hem at center front and mark with safety pin through both layers. Check doll in sitting position to allow for adequate ease in shirt, adjusting pin as needed; mark placement and remove pins. Remove the shirt.

2. Cut out 1"-wide wedge of center front and center back, from bottom to mark (Diagram 1). Turn shirt.

1"-WIDE OPENING

Diagram 1

3. Cut two 7" pieces of elastic. Thread through hem of each leg. Pin ends at raw edges. Turn shirt. Stitch inseam, securing elastic.

4. Cut out 1"-wide wedge 6" deep in center back at neck (Diagram 2). Fold raw edges double to wrong side and stitch with narrow hem. Attach closure, overlapping neck by 1".

1"-WIDE OPENING

Diagram 2

5. Place scrap paper inside shirt. Stencil star at center front. Allow to dry. Cut two 18" pieces of ribbon. Tie one at each wrist.

6. Tie remaining ribbon in bow on doll head. Fold tinsel double and thread around ribbon on front.

DIRECTIONS for Doll #2

1. Place shirt on doll. Pin a 1" to 1½"-deep tuck in back at neckline. Mark tail of shirt about mid-thigh on doll. Cut shirt tail off at

mark. Measure doll leg (Diagram 3). Subtract 1"

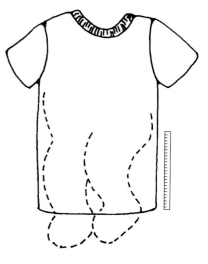

Diagram 3

from this measurement. Cut off this much from tail of second shirt (Diagram 4). Remove shirt. Aligning the raw edges, stitch the shirt tails together.

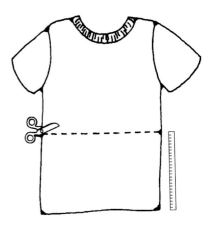

Diagram 4

2. Complete Steps 1 and 2 of Doll #1, then Step 4.

3. Place scrap paper inside shirt. Stencil one large yellow star and three small pink stars. Add yellow brush strokes as desired.

4. To make wig, measure circumference of doll head. Cut one wig from foam, adjusting as needed. Wrap yarn loosely in figure-8s around two fingers; do not cut end. Stitch center of loop to edge of foam (Diagram 5).

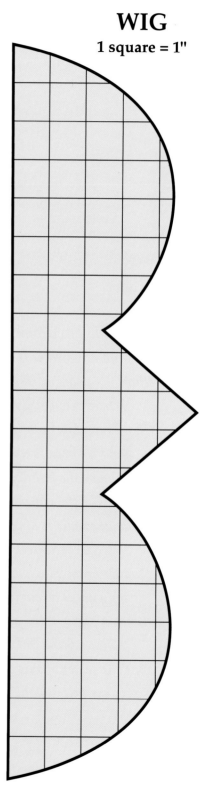

WIG
1 square = 1"

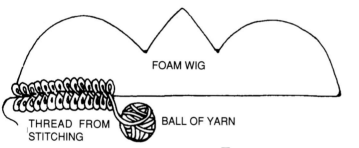

FOAM WIG

THREAD FROM STITCHING

BALL OF YARN

Diagram 5

Continue wrapping and stitching to complete one row. Repeat to complete second row 1" above first. Place wig on doll with ends of foam meeting at center back. Whipstitch ends together. Shape top edges to meet across crown of head; whipstitch. Remove the wig.

5. Stitch two 15" edges of netting together, leaving an opening. Turn. Place seam at center back over wig with 1" of netting over yarn loops. Stitch netting to wig. (This row of stitching is ¼" above second row of yarn. Do not catch yarn in seam under netting.) Place wig on doll and fold cuff in lower edge of netting. Twist netting into loose knots toward face; see photo. Tack. Tie cording around head. Cut loops of yarn and trim as desired.

Chapter Two
EVERY DAY'S
A
CELEBRATION!

Every day's a celebration,
    And nowhere is it more clear
Than the pages of this chapter,
    Where personalities will appear.
There's an angel who sparkles,
    And a sorceress who's bewitched,
But maybe the bridal gown
    Will be the one you choose to stitch.
A handkerchief is almost all you need
    For Sweet Sixteen's dress,
And Oriental Blossom's kimono,
    only needs a few tucks, we confess.
What a party in the garden;
    What a beautiful winter gown,
But the secret of this chapter
    Is the briefs—the best in town!

Basic Fashion Doll Dress

FABRIC

★ ¼ yard; see project:
   Two bodice fronts
   Four bodice backs
   Two sleeves
   One 24" x 9" skirt

MATERIALS

★ 6" of ⅛"-wide elastic
★ Closures
★ Matching thread

DIRECTIONS

1. Stitch darts in bodice fronts. Stitch one bodice front to two bodice backs at shoulders. Repeat with remaining bodice front and bodice backs. Place right sides of two bodices together, matching shoulder seams. Stitch along one center back seam, around neck and along second center back. Clip curved seam allowances of neck. Turn. Proceed to handle both layers of fabric as one.

2. Stitch narrow hem in wrist edge of one sleeve. Cut elastic in half. Stitch one piece of elastic ½" above hem. Stitch gathering threads along sleeve cap; gather to fit armhole. Stitch sleeve cap to bodice. Repeat.

3. Stitch side seam from bottom of bodice to hem of sleeve, adjusting elastic to fit doll and securing it in seam. Repeat.

4. Fold skirt with right sides together and short ends matching. Stitch short ends to within 2" of top edge; backstitch. (This seam is the center back; the long edge with the opening is the waist.) Fold edges of opening double to wrong side and stitch with a narrow hem.

5. Stitch gathering threads along waist of skirt. Make ½"-deep hem on opposite long edge. Match center fronts and gather skirt to fit bodice; stitch. Zigzag over raw edges of seam allowances at waistline. Attach closures.

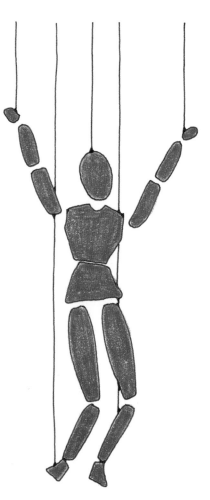

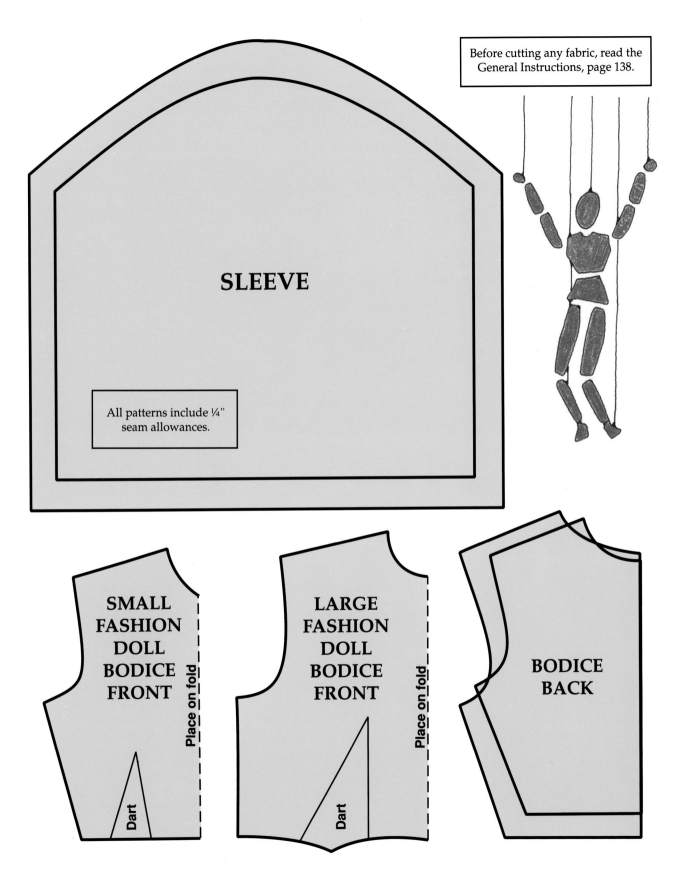

SLEEVE

All patterns include ¼"
seam allowances.

Before cutting any fabric, read the
General Instructions, page 138.

SMALL
FASHION
DOLL
BODICE
FRONT

Place on fold

Dart

LARGE
FASHION
DOLL
BODICE
FRONT

Place on fold

Dart

BODICE
BACK

Fashion Doll

Angel Dust and Sparkles

FABRICS

★ ¼ yard of white satin:
  Two bodice fronts*
  Four bodice backs*
  Two sleeves*
  One 24" x 9" skirt
★ ⅜ yard of white lace fabric:
  Seven 10" x 10" squares
  Five 7" x 7" squares
  One 3" x 3" square
  One 2" x 2" square
* Patterns on page 55.

MATERIALS

★ 1½ yards of ¼"-wide gold trim
★ Eight 5"-long white feathers
★ One 3" x 3" piece of stiff netting or horsehair
★ Glue gun and glue
★ Closures
★ Matching thread

DIRECTIONS

1. Complete Steps 1 through 5 of Basic Fashion Doll Dress, omitting elastic in sleeves.

2. Fold each 10" x 10" square into quarters to find center. Tack centers to waist of dress, spaced evenly and letting folds fall freely. Repeat with five 7" x 7" squares, tacking over large squares. Repeat with 3" x 3" squares at neckline of center front of dress. Attach smallest square over center front square.

3. Tack one row of gold trim to neckline. Tack two rows to wrist of both sleeves spaced ¼" apart. Wrap trim around waist three times, leaving 10" tails. Tie tails into a bow at the back.

4. To make wings, weave ends of feathers through horsehair or netting, placing four on each side (Diagram 1).

Tack to center back of dress. Cut one 12" piece of gold trim. Fold in half, placing fold at center back waist. Glue over center of wings. Wrap ends around front of dress and under arms to wings; glue ends to wings.

5. To style hair, put into ponytail on crown of head. Divide into seven equal amounts. Braid each and wrap in loop to base of ponytail; glue. Thread gold braid through loops of hair two times; glue ends of braid together.

Diagram 1

Fashion Doll
Oriental Blossom

FABRICS

★ Scrap of print:
   Two kimono fronts
   Two kimono backs
   Two sleeves
   One 2½" x 11½"
      obi (belt)
★ Scrap of different
   print:
   Two 4½" x 13" sleeve
      drapes
★ Scrap of different
   print:
   One train
   One 1¾" x 18"
      train tie
★ Scrap of purple satin:
   One 1" x 20" bias strip

MATERIALS

★ One 1" x 1¼" piece of
   lightweight cardboard
★ 2 yards of variegated
   pink thread
★ Matching threads

DIRECTIONS

1. Stitch two kimono backs together at center back. Stitch two kimono fronts to kimono back at shoulders. Stitch narrow hem in wrist edge of one sleeve. Stitch sleeve cap of one sleeve to armhole. Repeat. Stitch side seam from bottom of kimono to hem of the sleeve. Repeat.

2. Bind edge of kimono front opening and neck with bias strip.

3. Fold obi, matching long edges and with right sides together. Stitch ends and long edge, leaving 2" opening in center of long edge. Clip corners. Turn. Insert cardboard and center inside obi. Slipstitch opening closed. Topstitch through all layers to secure cardboard. Wrap variegated thread around center of obi in a double layer; glue ends at back. Wrap around waist of kimono and tie knot at center back.

4. Fold one sleeve drape with right sides together, matching long edges. Stitch edges, leaving an opening. Clip corners. Turn. Drape over one sleeve; slipstitch to top of sleeve to secure. Slipstitch front edges together on lower 3".

5. Stitch narrow hem in sides and bottom edges of train. Pin six tucks in top edge; see pattern. Topstitch tucks. Fold train tie with wrong sides together, matching long edges. Stitch edges, leaving 2" opening in center. Insert top of train in opening. Slipstitch opening closed, securing train in stitches. Tie train to back of doll with knot at center front of neck.

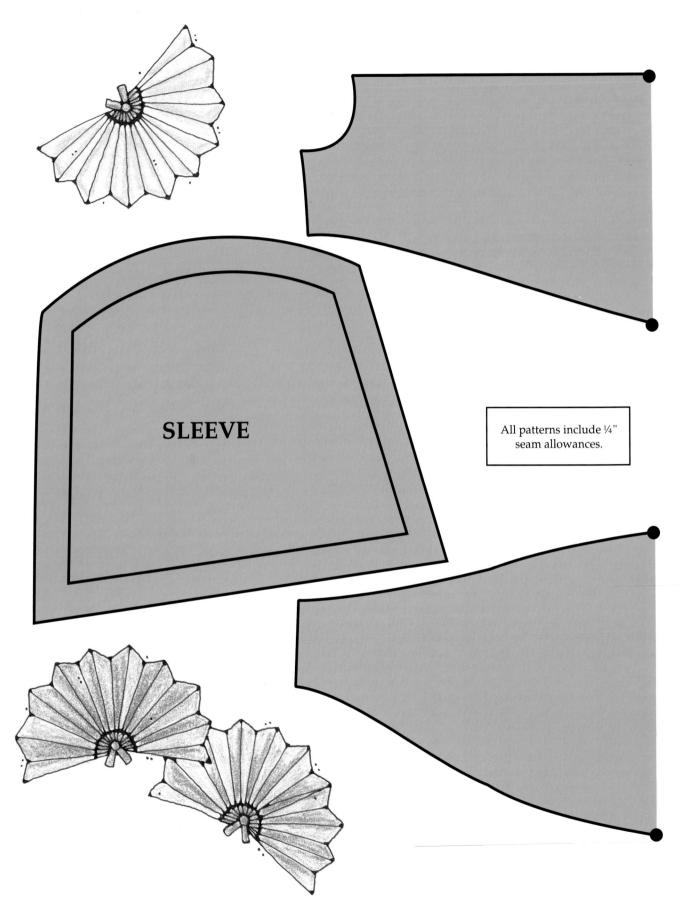

SLEEVE

All patterns include ¼"
seam allowances.

Center back

KIMONO BACK

Match patterns at each dot

Cut here for small doll

Cut here for large doll

Before cutting any fabric, read the
General Instructions, page 138.

KIMONO FRONT

Match patterns at each dot

Cut here for small doll

Cut here for large doll

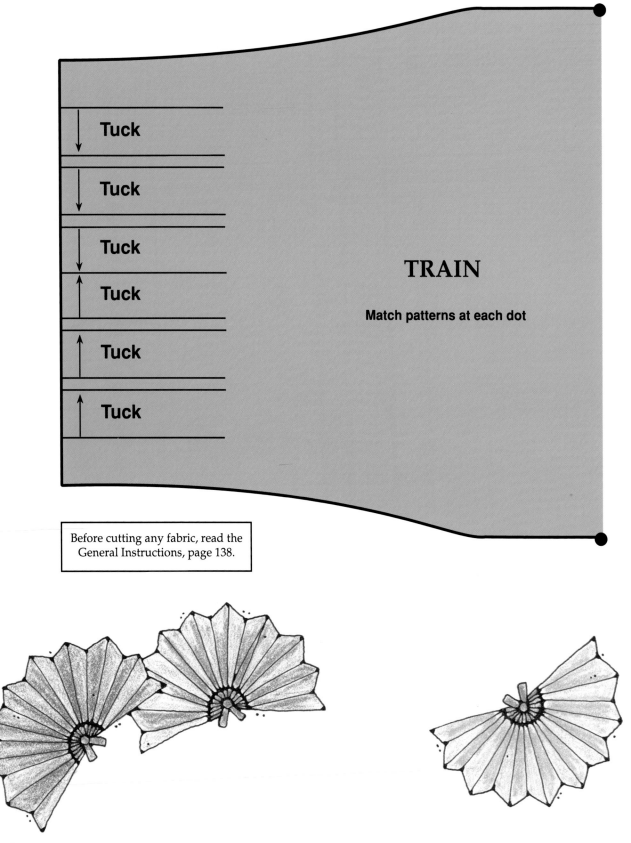

Tuck

Tuck

Tuck

Tuck

Tuck

Tuck

TRAIN

Match patterns at each dot

Before cutting any fabric, read the
General Instructions, page 138.

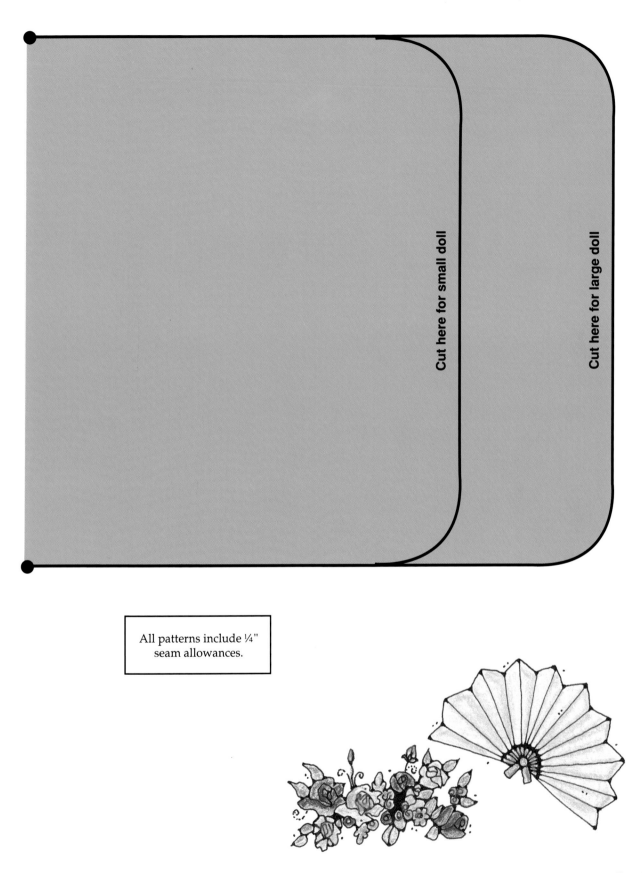

Cut here for small doll

Cut here for large doll

All patterns include ¼"
seam allowances.

Garden Tea Party

FABRIC

★ ³⁄₈ yard of green satin:
Two bodice fronts*
Four bodice backs*
Two sleeves
Two cuffs
One skirt center front**
Two skirt side fronts**
Two skirt side backs**
Two skirt backs**
One crown; see Step 10
* Patterns on page 55.
** Note notches in skirt
pieces.

MATERIALS

★ 13 yards of ¾"-wide
gathered green lace
★ One 4½"-wide
mesh hat
★ 18 apricot ribbon
flowers
★ 18 blue ribbon flowers
★ 15 green ribbon leaves
★ 1¼ yards of iridescent
green craft beads
★ Closures
★ Matching threads

DIRECTIONS

1. Mark parallel lines ¼"
and ½" below neck on one
bodice front. Cut one 4" and
one 6" piece of lace. Remove
gathering threads from lace.
Regather to fit front neck of
dress. Stitch 6" piece on line
½" below neck (Diagram 1).
Stitch 4" piece on ¼" line.

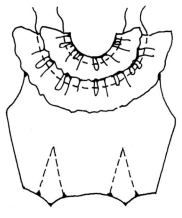

Diagram 1

2. Stitch darts in bodice
fronts. Stitch one bodice
front to two bodice backs at
shoulders, securing ends of
lace in seams. Repeat with
remaining bodice front and
backs. Place right sides of
two bodices together,
matching shoulder seams.
Stitch along one center

back, around neck and
along second center back.
Clip curved edges. Turn.
Proceed to handle both
layers of fabric as one.

3. Place one sleeve on flat
surface and mark six parallel rows ½" apart, beginning
¾" above wrist edge. Stitch
gathered lace to rows,
beginning on wrist edge
and overlapping. Repeat.
(Many laces such as that
used on this dress come
with a sheer binding on the
gathered edge. In attaching
such lace to the sleeves and
skirt, stitch the lace just
below the edge of the binding. At the end of each row,
release the chain stitch that
has secured the binding and
gathers and discard. This
reduces the bulk at the top
edge of the lace.)

4. Stitch gathering threads in sleeve cap and wrist edge of one sleeve. Gather wrist to fit cuff. Fold cuff with wrong sides together. Stitch cuff to wrist edge of sleeve. Gather sleeve cap to fit armhole. Stitch sleeve to armhole without catching edges of lace on bodice front. Repeat.

5. Stitch side seam from bottom of bodice to cuff of sleeve. Repeat.

6. Stitch skirt side front to skirt center front along side edges. Press seam allowance open. Zigzag bottom edge. Fold edge under ¼". Stitch gathered lace to edge. Stitch two rows of lace ½" apart and parallel to bottom edge. Set skirt front aside.

7. Stitch skirt side backs to skirt backs, matching notches. Stitch center back to within 2" of top edge; backstitch. (This seam is the center back; the long edge with the opening is the waist.) Fold edges of opening double to wrong side and stitch. Press all seam allowances in skirt open. Mark twenty intervals ½" apart on center back seam with one ¼" below waist and one ⅜" above bottom edge. Zigzag bottom edges. Fold edge under ¼". Stitch gathered lace to edge.

Continue to attach lace on parallel rows, following contour of hemline and working around center back opening at waist, until all of skirt back is covered.

8. Stitch skirt front to skirt back. Stitch gathering threads around waist of skirt. Match center fronts and gather skirt, except at center front, to fit the bodice; stitch together. Attach the closures.

9. Cut one 4" strand of beads; tie in a bow and attach to neckline. Attach four apricot flowers, four blue flowers and eight green leaves to waist/skirt seam at center front of dress. Cut one 12" strand of beads; weave through flowers and arrange as desired. Cut one 8" strand of beads. Tack to bottom front of dress where lace and satin meet. Attach two apricot flowers, two blue flowers, and three green leaves to bottom corner where lace and satin meet. Cut one 4" strand of beads; weave through flowers and arrange as desired. Repeat at opposite corner.

HAT

10. Measure crown of hat. Glue satin crown over crown of hat. Glue lace to outside edge of hat on top and bottom of brim. Continue to glue four additional overlapping rows until both sides are covered.

11. Attach nine apricot flowers, eleven blue flowers and eighteen green leaves around crown and on top of brim of hat. Cut one 18" strand of beads; weave through flowers and arrange as desired.

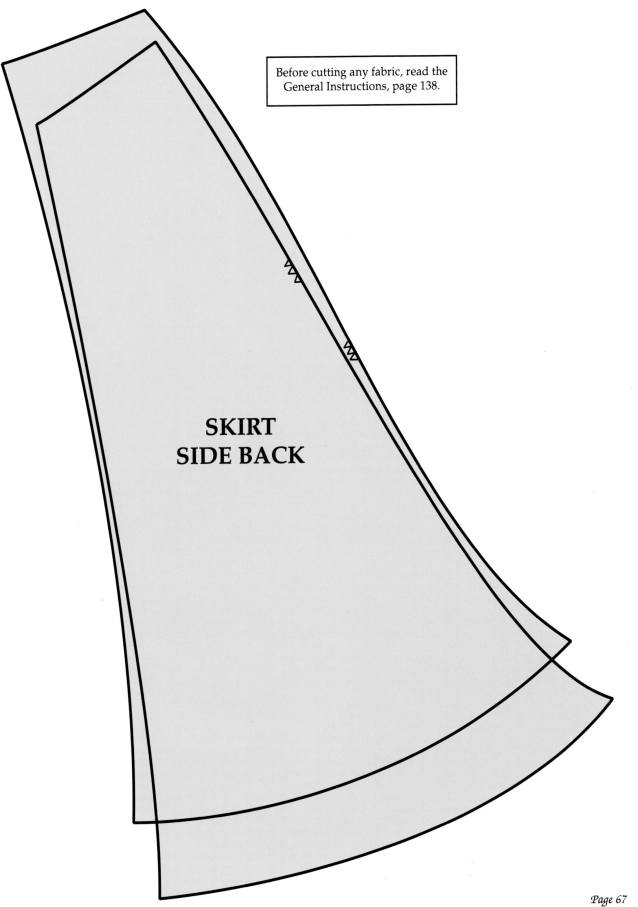

Before cutting any fabric, read the
General Instructions, page 138.

**SKIRT
SIDE BACK**

SLEEVE

All patterns include ¼"
seam allowances.

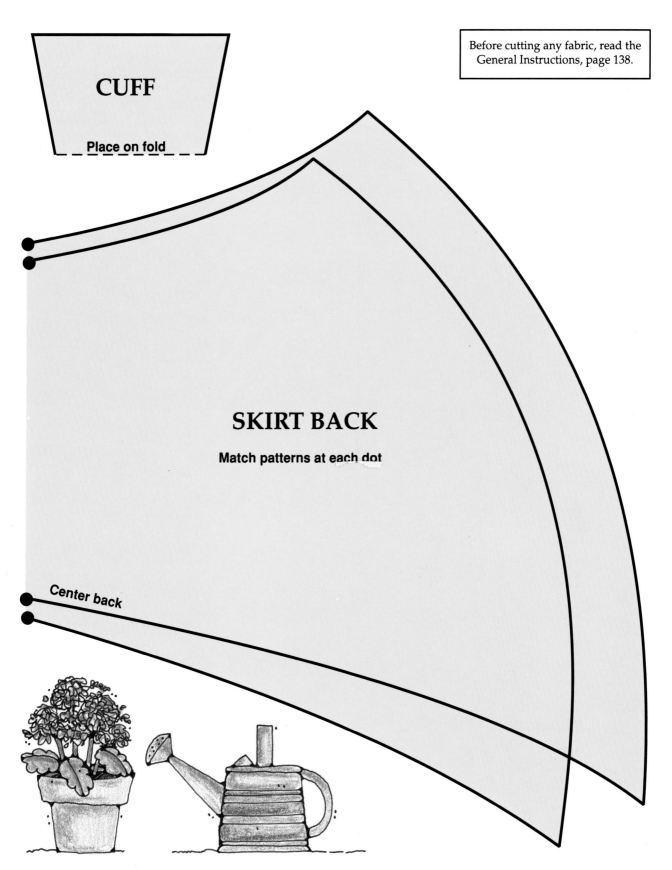

CUFF

Place on fold

Before cutting any fabric, read the General Instructions, page 138.

SKIRT BACK

Match patterns at each dot

Center back

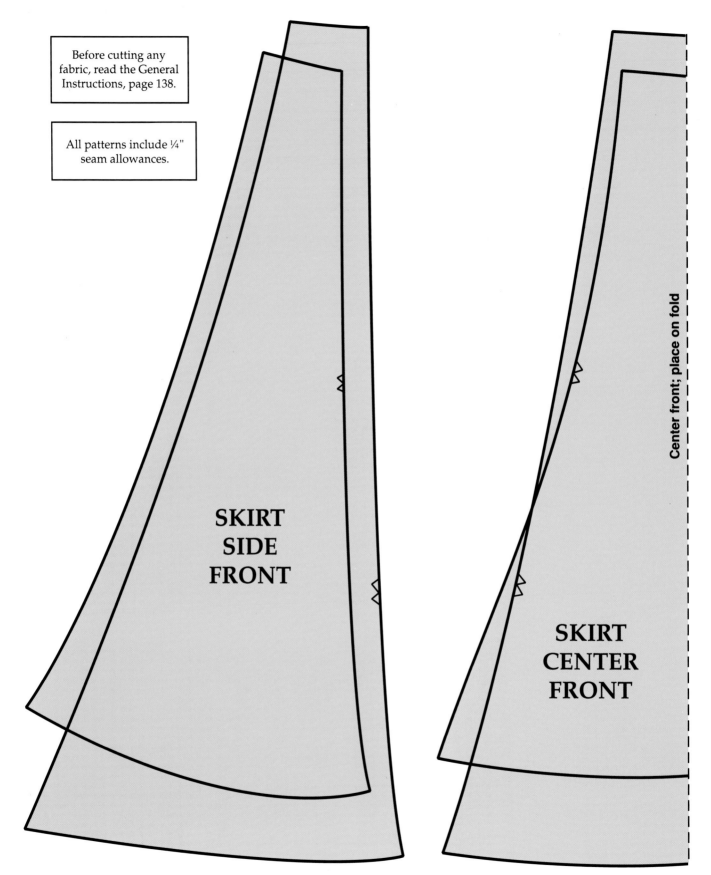

Before cutting any fabric, read the General Instructions, page 138.

All patterns include ¼" seam allowances.

SKIRT SIDE FRONT

SKIRT CENTER FRONT

Center front; place on fold

Fashion Doll

Petals and Pearls Bride

FABRICS

★ ½ yard of white satin:
Two bodice fronts*
Four bodice backs*
Two sleeves**
Two cuffs***
Two collars
One skirt center front***
Two skirt side fronts***
Two skirt side backs***
Two skirt backs***
★ ¼ yard of white tulle:
Two 9" x 15" pieces
*Patterns on page 55.
**Pattern on page 68.
***Note notches on skirt
  pieces. Patterns on
  pages 67, 68, 69 and 70.

MATERIALS

★ 1¼ yards of ¼"-wide
  silver/white ribbon
★ Six sprays of white
  organdy and satin
  flowers in two or
  three sizes
★ Closures
★ Matching thread

DIRECTIONS

1. Stitch darts in bodice fronts. Stitch one bodice front to two bodice backs at shoulders. Repeat with remaining bodice front and backs. Place two collar pieces with right sides together. Stitch ends and inside curved edge. Clip corners. Turn. Mark centers of collar and neck front. Match with right sides together, carefully pinning curves against each other. Baste collar to neck of bodice. Place right sides of two bodices together, matching shoulder seams. Stitch along one center back, around neck (securing collar) and along second

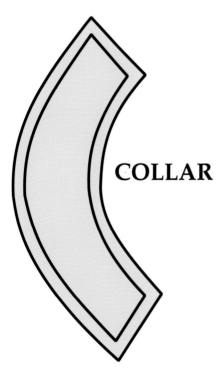

COLLAR

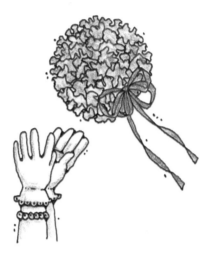

center back. Clip curved edges. Turn. Proceed to handle both layers of bodice as one.

2. Stitch gathering threads in sleeve cap and wrist edge of one sleeve. Gather wrist to fit cuff. Fold cuff with wrong sides together. Stitch cuff to wrist edge of sleeve. Gather sleeve to fit armhole. Stitch sleeve cap to bodice. Repeat.

3. Stitch skirt side front to skirt center front along side edges. Then stitch skirt side backs to skirt, matching notches. Stitch skirt backs to skirt, matching notches. Stitch center back to within 2" of top edge; backstitch. (This seam is the center back; the long edge with the opening is the waist.) Fold edges of opening double to wrong side and stitch. Press all of the seam allowances in skirt open.

4. Stitch gathering threads around the waist of skirt. Stitch narrow hem in bottom edge of skirt. Match center fronts and gather skirt, except at center front, to fit bodice; stitch together. Attach closures.

5. Sew running stitch in one 9" edge of each tulle piece. Gather tightly and secure thread. Sew running stitches around remaining edges of tulle on each piece. Pull tightly, tucking gathered edges under side. Tack tulle to waist of dress on each side.

6. Shape one spray of flowers into a wreath. Tie ribbon into six to eight loops and attach to wreath. Tack larger stems to center back and below tulle pieces, hairpiece and wreath. Cut apart remaining sprays as desired and tack to dress, placing smallest flowers on hem and over one shoulder. Add pearls (from flower sprays) to neck of dress. Tie ribbon into six or eight loops and attach to wreath.

Fashion Doll

Sultry Sorceress

DIRECTIONS

1. Complete Steps 1 through 5 of Basic Fashion Doll Dress, omitting hem in sleeves and skirt and elastic in sleeve.

2. Prepare four containers of paint for dying cheesecloth, mixing paint and water in equal quantities. From cheesecloth, cut one 6" x 24" piece and six 6" x 12" pieces; dye brown. Cut one 12" x 12" piece and nine 6" x 12" pieces; dye purple. Cut five 6" x 12" pieces; dye red. Cut five 6" x 12" pieces;

dye blue. Spread cheesecloth on newspaper to dry, allowing folds in the fabric to create irregular patterns.

3. Put dress on doll. Cut 2" to 4" irregular slashes in hems of dress and sleeves.

4. Using black thread, sew running stitches in one 6" edge of each blue piece of cheesecloth; secure thread. Pin gathered ends to waist of dress, placing one at center back and two spaced evenly on front. (You may wish to remove the dress as you attach each layer, or you may wish to tack the layers on the dressed doll.) Tack gathered ends. Use hands to tear holes in cheesecloth and to shred ends.

5. Gather one end of one red and two purple 6" x 12" pieces. Tack red piece at center front and purple pieces between blue pieces. Tear and shred. Gather one 24" edge of brown piece. Tack loosely over first layer of cheesecloth. Tear and shred.

6. Fold one purple 6" x 12" piece to measure 6" x 6". Gather folded edge to 3". Tack to front neckline of dress to resemble bib. Tack one corner of two red pieces to each side of back neckline. Knot opposite corners. Tack one corner of two remaining red pieces to each shoulder. Also tack tucks in cheesecloth and sleeves inside elbows to gather sleeves slightly. Shred, tear and knot cheesecloth.

7. Put doll hair in ponytail. Cut one headdress from Paperform. Heat at 200° in oven until soft. Place diagonal edge of headdress over doll face and mold to fit head, folding pleats to outside (Diagram 1). Allow to cool. Place outside of mold on fabric headdress near one corner. Fold cor-

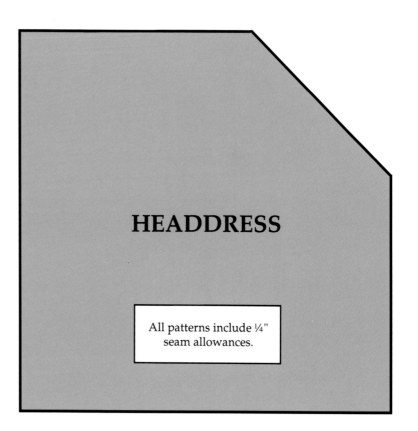

HEADDRESS

All patterns include ¼" seam allowances.

ners of fabric over headdress (Diagram 2). Glue. Drape fabric over right side of mold. Shred edges.

8. Glue one corner of four 6" x 12" brown pieces of cheesecloth to diagonal edge of headdress. Knot

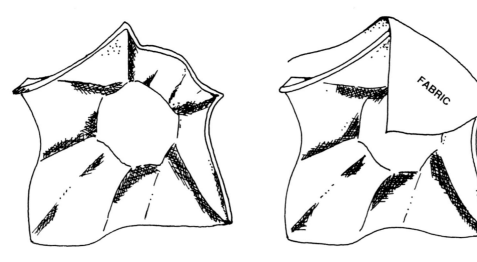

Diagram 1

Diagram 2

ends. Glue one end of two 6" x 12" purple pieces to inside front of headdress (below ears). Knot ends.

9. Cut five ½" x 4" strips from Paperform. Wrapping from one end of 12" x 12" purple piece of cheesecloth, twist fabric around one strip of Paperform. Wrap strip/fabric around pencil, secure both ends of Paperform with a rubber band, letting remainder of cheesecloth drape (Diagram 3). Repeat with four 6" x 12" purple pieces and remaining Paperform strips. Glue to back of headdress. Twist remaining brown piece and glue to top of forehead.

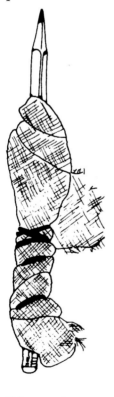

Diagram 3

Fashion Doll

Sixteen Candles

FABRICS	MATERIALS

FABRICS

★ ¼ yard of cream linen:
   One dress front
   Two dress backs
   Two sleeves
★ Scrap of print:
   Two 1½" x 1" wrist
      bindings

MATERIALS

★ One 10" x 10" white
   linen handkerchief
   with decorative motif
   in one corner
★ ⅜ yard of cream
   ribbon with gold
   edging
★ Closures
★ Matching thread
★ Dressmakers' pen

DIRECTIONS

1. Stitch dress front to dress backs at shoulders.

2. Stitch four 1"-long ¼"-deep tucks in wrist of sleeve. Bind wrist edges. Stitch gathering threads along sleeve cap; gather to fit armhole. Stitch sleeve cap to dress. Repeat.

3. Stitch side seam from bottom of dress to hem wrist edge of sleeve. Repeat. Stitch center back seam to within 4" of neck. Stitch narrow hem on bottom edge of dress. Turn dress.

4. Cut handkerchief into square quarters (Diagram 1).

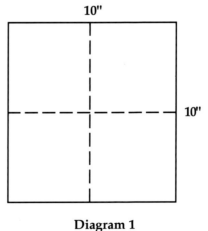

Diagram 1

5. Measure diameter of neck opening of dress Cut out a circle this size from center of square with decorative motif. Starting at corner opposite motif, make a diagonal slit from corner to circle (Diagram 2).

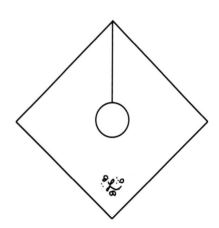

Diagram 2

Stitch narrow hem in outside raw edges. With motif centered at front, and with right side of handkerchief against wrong side of bodice, stitch circle to neck of dress with small stitches and a narrow seam. Clip curved edges. Turn collar to front of dress. Fold side corners under and tack points to shoulders.

6. Measure and mark around dress 2¾" above hem. Stitch gathering threads along 2¾" mark. Gather to equal 7"; stitch on line to secure gathers.

7. Stitch gathering threads diagonally along three remaining squares (Diagram 3).

Cut off one corner of square ¼" from threads. Matching gathering threads of one square and dress, pin with point facing center top of dress and with right sides together (Diagram 4).

Diagram 4

Repeat, placing two remaining quarters on dress, aligning points with side seams and meeting at center back. Gather handkerchief pieces slightly. Stitch to secure, sewing on gathering line of dress. Fold down squares. Attach closures. Make a 4"-wide bow from ribbon. Attach to center back where squares meet dress.

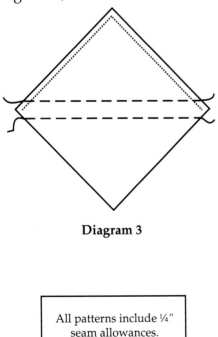

Diagram 3

All patterns include ¼"
seam allowances.

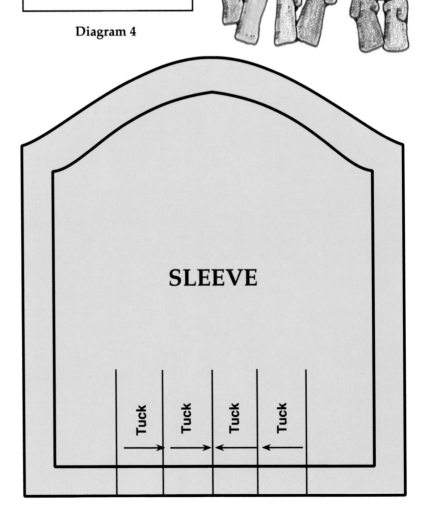

SLEEVE

Tuck   Tuck   Tuck   Tuck

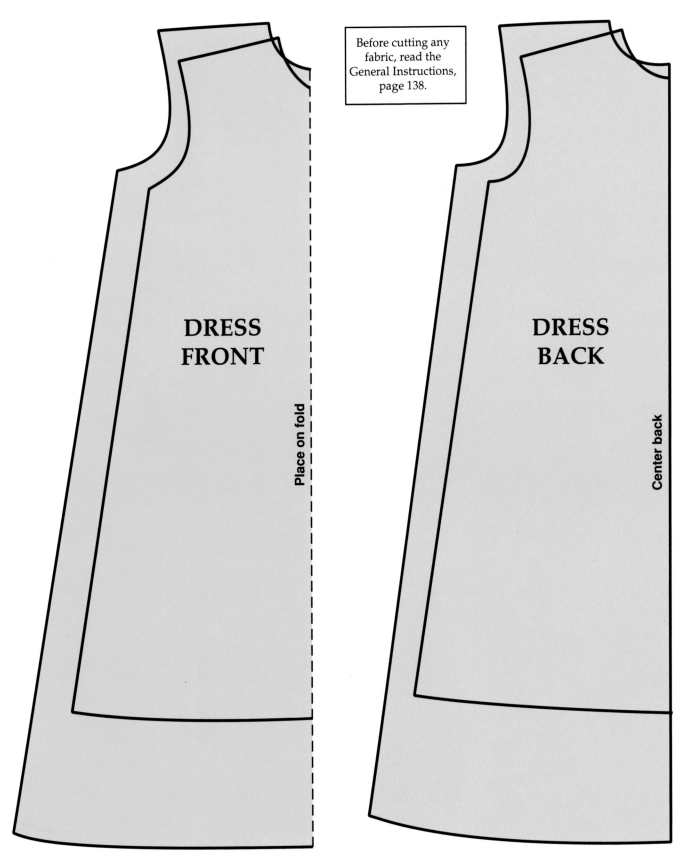

DRESS
FRONT

Place on fold

DRESS
BACK

Center back

Before cutting any
fabric, read the
General Instructions,
page 138.

Fashion Doll

Winter's Precious Wonder

FABRICS

★ ⅝ yard of dark green velvet:
  Two bodice fronts*
  Four bodice backs*
  Two sleeves**
  Two cuffs**
  One collar*
  One skirt center front**
  Two skirt side fronts**
  Two skirt side backs**
  Two skirt backs**
  One cape back
  Two cape fronts
  One hat
★ ¼ yard of silk batting:
  One muff
  Trim; see Steps 3 and 4

★ ⅜ yard of dark green taffeta:
  One cape back
  Two cape fronts
  One collar*

  *Patterns on pages 55 and 73.
  ** Note notches on skirt pieces. Patterns on pages 67, 68, 69 and 70.

MATERIALS

★ One hook and eye
★ Metallic gold thread
★ Closures
★ Matching thread

DIRECTIONS

1. Complete Steps 1 through 4 of Petals and Pearls Bride using green velvet fabric.

2. To make cape, stitch fronts to back on side seam. Repeat with taffeta fronts and back. Match two capes at side seams. Stitch all outside edges, leaving an opening. Clip curved seam allowances. Turn. Slipstitch opening closed. Sew running stitches around neck close to seam. Gather slightly. Secure threads.

3. Separate batting into strands. Whipstitch to edge of cape taking stitches ½" apart. Also whipstitch batting to hem of dress. Brush batting slightly to make "furry." Attach hook and eye at neck of cape.

HAT AND MUFF

4. Sew running stitch around edge of hat circle. Gather to fit doll head; secure thread. Couch silk batting to edge, using gold thread.

5. Glue ends together. Whipstitch edges of muff, using gold thread.

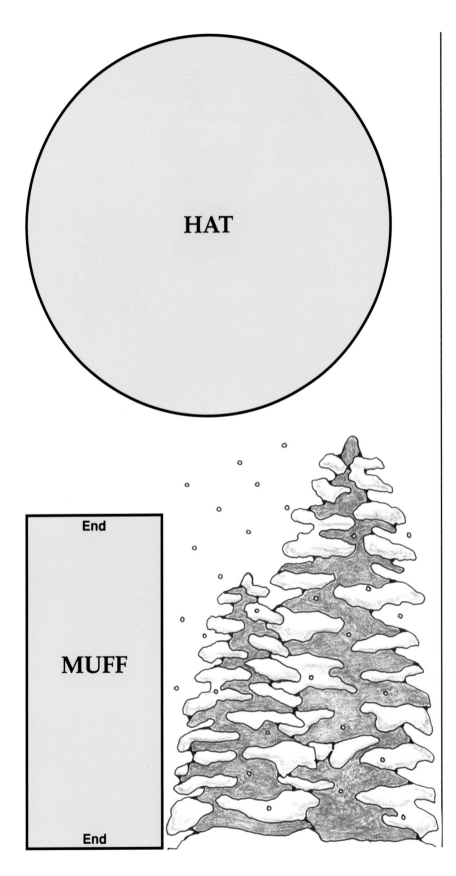

HAT

End

MUFF

End

DID YOU KNOW. . .

Winter is the coldest season of the year. It begins at the winter solstice, the year's shortest day, and ends at the vernal equinox, when day and night are equally long. Winter is marked by low temperatures, snowfalls, cold waves, and reduced sunlight.

The muff, a separate, pillow-like or tubular covering for hands worn for warmth, came into being the end of the 16th century, specifically to combat those cold wintery days and nights. The muff has historically been constructed from woolen fabric, feathers or fur. It is now worn chiefly by women and children. However, muffs were carried by men in the United States as late as the 18th century.

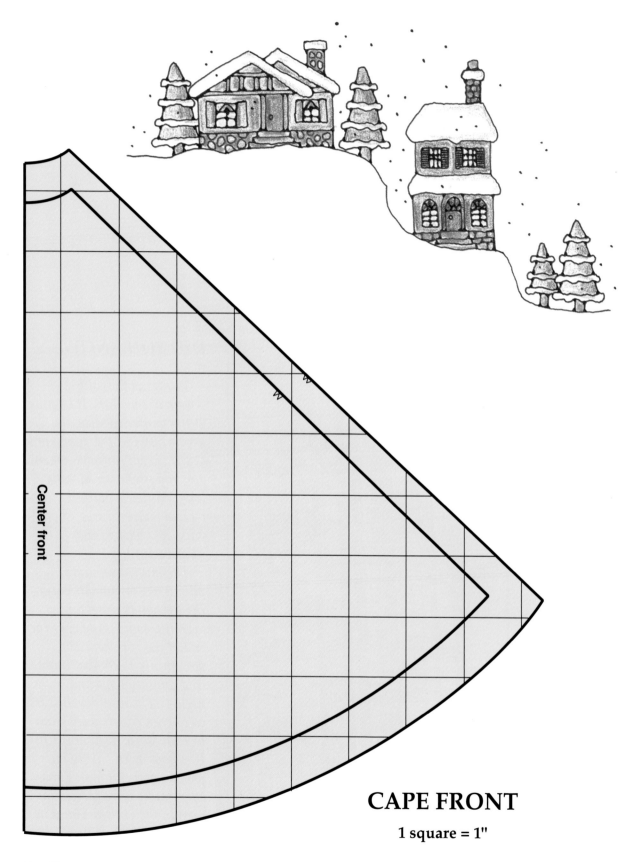

Center front

CAPE FRONT

1 square = 1"

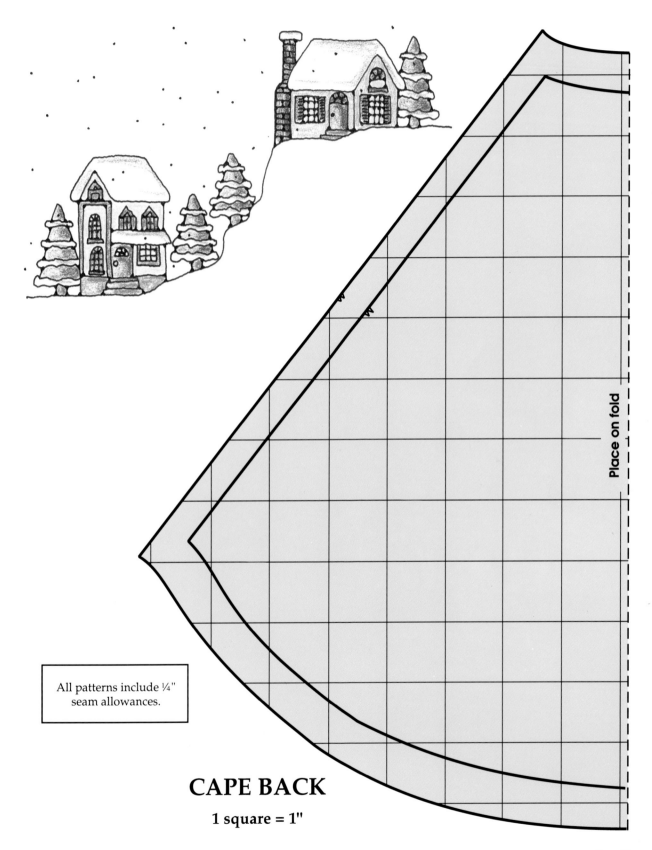

All patterns include ¼"
seam allowances.

Place on fold

CAPE BACK

1 square = 1"

Autumn Forest Fairy

FABRIC

★ ¼ yard of apricot:
Two bodice fronts*
Four bodice backs*
Two sleeves*
One 24" x 9" skirt
*Patterns on page 55.

MATERIALS

★ 6" of ⅛"-wide elastic
★ Four 7" x 7" cream lace squares
★ 1¼ yard of ½"-wide sheer silk ribbon
★ Two 2"-wide butterfly appliques
★ Dried leaves
★ Opaque flower buttons
★ Several small plastic leaves
★ One small plastic bird
★ Twelve cream beads
★ One ornament that resembles a lantern
★ Two small buttons
★ Glue gun and glue
★ Closures
★ Matching threads

DIRECTIONS

1. Complete Steps 1 through 5 of Basic Fashion Doll Dress using apricot fabric. Do not hem dress.

2. Tack wrong side of one corner of one lace square to center front of dress at waist. Tack two additional pieces to waist in back, spaced evenly. Tack bottom corner of each lace piece to lower edge of dress. Trim apricot skirt to generally match edges of lace squares.

3. From fourth lace piece, cut two pieces about 2" x 6", depending upon design in lace. Also cut one about 1½" x 3". Tack wrong side of small piece to bodice front, placing top edge horizontally 1¾" above waist. Place larger pieces over each shoulder, tacking at center back and under each arm to form a shawl.

4. Tie sheer silk ribbon in a bow around hair. Glue beads and two small but-

tons to bow. Tack two small branches to back of dress. Glue butterflies to branches. Cut two 4" pieces of green ribbon. Wrap around wrist over dress; tack. Wrap remaining ribbon around waist, folding three deep loops; tack. Thread flower buttons, leaves and bird onto threads of varied lengths; tack to waist near bow. Place ornament in hand. Add one or two small dried leaves to hair.

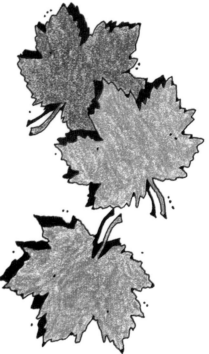

Fashion Doll

Peek-a-Boo Briefs

FABRICS

★ Scraps of white lace
   or tricot:
   One bra
   One panties
★ ½ yard of white:
   One 15"-wide circle

MATERIALS

★ 5" of ¼"-wide white
   satin ribbon
★ 3" of ⅛"-wide elastic
★ 15" of ¼"-wide flat
   white lace
★ One ¼" x ¼" piece
   of hook and loop tape
★ 3" of ⅛"-wide elastic
★ ⅜ yard of ½"-wide
   flat white trim
★ Matching thread

DIRECTIONS

1. To make bra, stitch lace
to all edges. Cut ribbon into
two equal pieces. Stitch
ends to bra where indi-
cated; see pattern. Stitch
hook and loop tape to
center back. Sew running
stitch through vertical
center. Gather; see photo.
Secure thread.

2. To make panties, stitch
lace to each leg edge. Stitch
elastic around waist. Stitch
center back, then crotch.

3. To make slip, cut
2"-wide circle for waist in
center of white circle. Stitch
elastic to waist. Stitch trim
to outside of slip, using
zigzag stitch to secure
raw edges.

All patterns include ¼"
seam allowances.

Before cutting any fabric, read the
General Instructions, page 138.

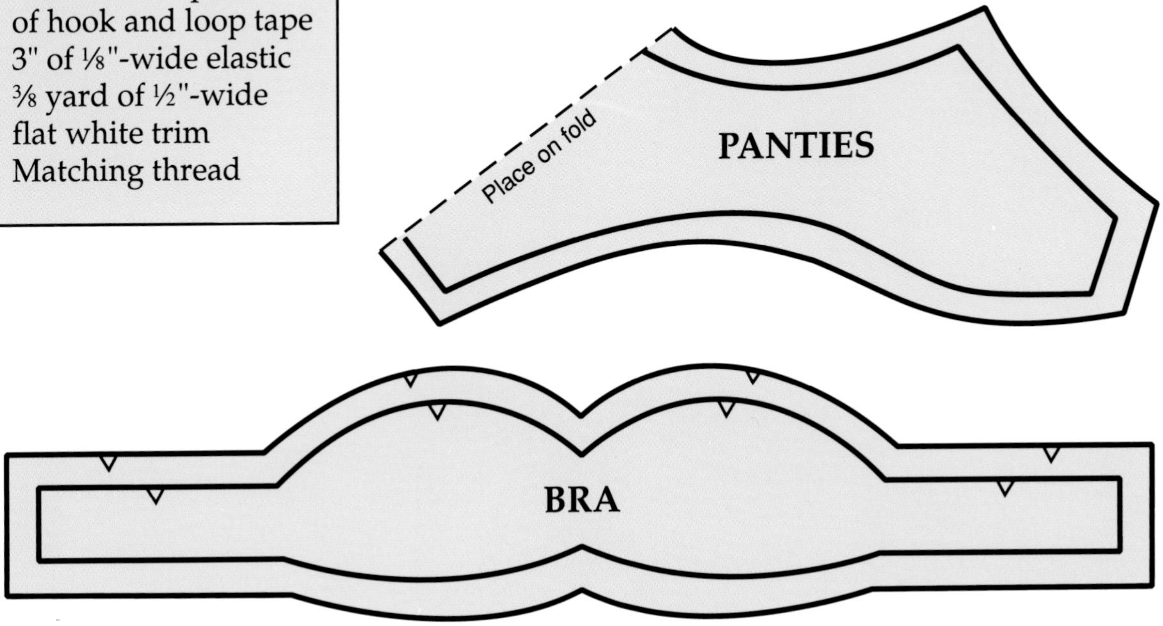

PANTIES

Place on fold

BRA

Chapter Three
TEACHER'S PETS
AND
SWEETIE PIES

Reading to Miss Kitty
    Is a pastime we adore,
Creating dolls with a Shakespearean flair,
    Is something we like more.
Don't forget dressing our princesses,
    Two to be precise,
And the cutie dressed in ruffles,
    Is a doll who looks so nice!
There's also a mystical magical,
    Charming masquerade,
And don't forget Puss 'n' Boots—
    not part of this decade.
So take a stroll through Chapter Three;
    It will make you start to dream.
Your daydreams may make you the one
    Who's dressed up as the queen.

Little Girl Doll

Basic Little Girl Dress

FABRIC

★ ¼ yard of fabric; see project:
   Two bodice fronts
   Four bodice backs
   Two sleeves
   One 9" x 34" skirt

MATERIALS

★ 6" of ⅛"-wide elastic
★ Closures
★ Matching thread

DIRECTIONS

1. Stitch one bodice front to two bodice backs at shoulders. Repeat with remaining bodice front and bodice backs. Place right sides of two bodices together, matching shoulder seams. Stitch along one center back, around neck and along second center back. Clip curved seam allowance of neck. Turn. Proceed to handle both layers of fabric as one.

2. Stitch narrow hem in wrist edge of one sleeve. Cut elastic in half. Stitch one piece of elastic ½" above hem. Stitch gathering threads along sleeve cap; gather to fit armhole. Stitch sleeve cap to bodice. Repeat.

3. Stitch side seam from bottom of bodice to hem of sleeve, adjusting elastic to fit doll and securing it in seam. Repeat.

4. Fold skirt with right sides together and short ends matching. Stitch short ends to within 2" of top edge; backstitch. (This seam is the center back; the long edge   the opening is the waist.) Fold edges of opening double to wrong side and stitch with a narrow hem.

5. Stitch gathering threads along waist of skirt. Make ½"-deep hem on opposite long edge. Match center fronts and gather skirt to fit bodice; stitch. Zigzag over raw edges of seam

allowances at waistline. Attach closures.

Before cutting any fabric, read the
General Instructions, page 138.

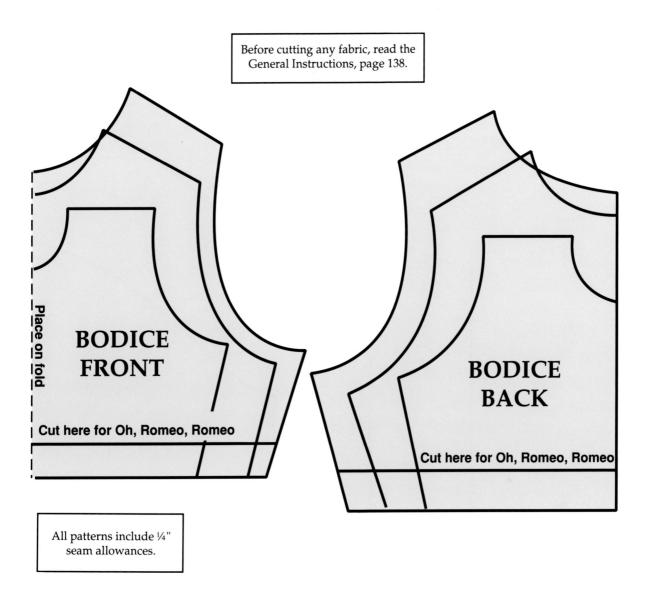

Place on fold

BODICE FRONT

Cut here for Oh, Romeo, Romeo

BODICE BACK

Cut here for Oh, Romeo, Romeo

All patterns include ¼"
seam allowances.

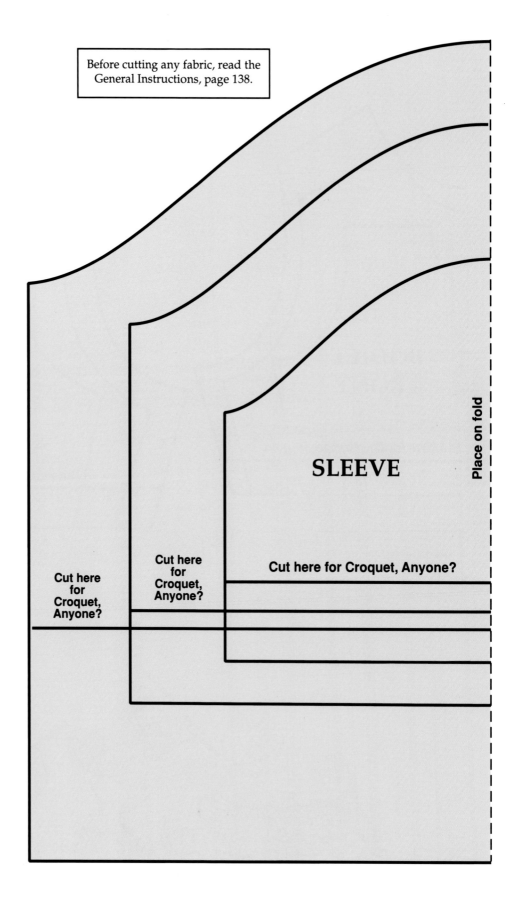

Before cutting any fabric, read the General Instructions, page 138.

SLEEVE

Place on fold

Cut here for Croquet, Anyone?

Cut here for Croquet, Anyone?

Cut here for Croquet, Anyone?

Little Girl Doll
Slips and Bloomers

FABRICS

★ ¼ yard of white batiste:
  Two bodice fronts*
  Four bodice backs*
  One 4" x 45" skirt
★ ¼ yard of lightweight fabric:
  Two pantalets

*Patterns on page 107.

MATERIALS

★ 1¼ yards of ⅝"-wide gathered white lace
★ ⅜ yard of ⅝"-wide flat white lace
★ 9" to 11" of ⅛"-wide elastic
★ Closures
★ Matching Thread

DIRECTIONS

1. To make slip, stitch one bodice front to two bodice backs at shoulders and side seams. Repeat with remaining bodice front and bodice backs. Place right sides of two bodices together, matching shoulder seams. Stitch along one center back seam, around neck and along second center back. Clip curved seam allowances of neck and armholes. Turn. Slipstitch the armholes closed.

2. Stitch narrow hem one long edge of skirt. Stitch gathered lace over hem on right side of skirt. Sew gathering threads on remaining long edge.

3. Match center fronts and gather skirt to fit bodice; stitch. Place flat lace over right side of seam at waist, aligning bottom edge of lace with seam. Topstitch both edges, folding ends under at center back. Attach the closures.

4. To make pantalets, stitch the center front and center back seams of the pantalets. Then stitch the inseam.

5. Make ½" casing at waist. Measure waist of doll. Cut piece of elastic the same as the measurement. Insert; overlap ends ½" and secure. Slipstitch opening closed. Stitch a narrow hem in each leg. Sew elastic ½" above each hemmed edge. Gather to fit doll and secure.

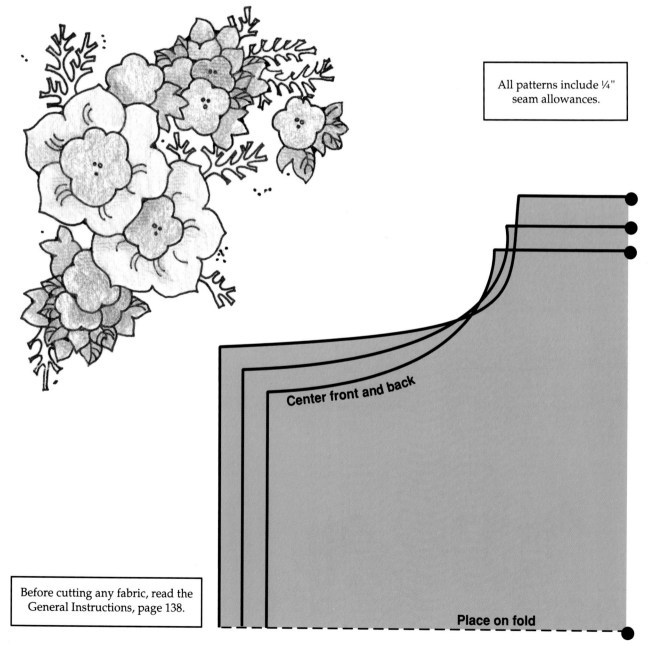

All patterns include ¼"
seam allowances.

Center front and back

Place on fold

Before cutting any fabric, read the
General Instructions, page 138.

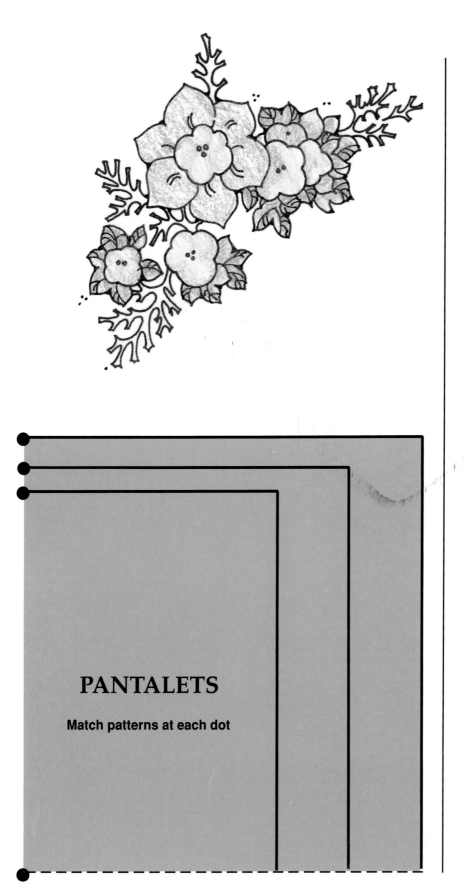

PANTALETS

Match patterns at each dot

DID YOU KNOW...

What is the difference between pantalets, pantaloons and bloomers?

Pantelets are long drawers extended below the skirt with a fullness or other finish at the bottom of the leg. Pantelets were commonly worn by women and girls in the 19th century.

A pantaloon is a man's close-fitting garment for the hips and legs, worn especially in the 19th century, but varying from period to period. The dictionary describes a pantaloon as another word for trouser.

Bloomers were part of a costume for women, advocated about 1850 by Amelia Jenks Bloomer. The costume consisted of a short skirt, loose trousers gathered and buttoned at the ankle, and often times, a coat and wide hat.

Reading to Miss Kitty

FABRIC

★ ¼ yard of cream:
Two bodice fronts*
Four bodice backs*
Two sleeves*
One 9" x 34" skirt
*Patterns on pages 95 and 96.

MATERIALS

★ 1⅛ yards of 5"-wide flat cream eyelet
★ 6" of ⅛"-wide elastic
★ ½ yard of ¼"-wide rose silk ribbon
★ Five ribbon roses
★ Closures
★ Matching thread

DIRECTIONS

1. Complete Step 1 of Basic Little Girl Dress. From eyelet, cut two 2¾" pieces and one 34" piece.

2. Overlap short eyelet pieces to make one piece with beading in center; trim excess (Diagram 1).

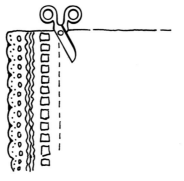

Diagram 1

Cut a 3" piece of ribbon; thread through beading. Center and stitch eyelet on bodice front (Diagram 2).

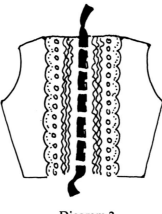

Diagram 2

Trim eyelet to edges of bodice front. Complete Steps 2 and 3 of Basic Little Girl Dress.

3. Complete Step 4 of Basic Little Girl Dress. Repeat with remaining eyelet. Place eyelet over dress skirt, matching center back seams and raw edges at waist. Complete Step 5 of Basic Little Girl Dress.

4. Cut one 34" piece of ribbon and thread into beading on skirt. Cut one 4½" piece of ribbon and tie into small bow. Tack bow to skirt; see photo. Tack ribbon roses over bow. Cut ribbon into two equal pieces. Tie around waist of the dress.

Miss Kitty's Overstuffed Chair

FABRIC

★ 1 yard of stripe:
  Two back sides
  Four arm sides
  One seat
  One 5½" x 5½"
    seat bottom
  One 5½" x 26" back
  Two 7" x 18" arms
  3½"-wide strips,
    against the grain of
    the fabric, piecing
    as needed to equal
    one 88" ruffle

MATERIALS

★ Buttonhole twist
  thread
★ Stuffing
★ Glue gun and glue
★ Long needle
★ Matching threads

DIRECTIONS

1. Stitch seat into a box shape by matching right sides of A to A and so on. With right sides together, stitch seat bottom to open edges, leaving an opening. Turn. Stuff firmly. Slipstitch opening closed.

2. Stitch back to all edges of one back side, beginning at bottom of back side and clipping seam allowance of back at corners (Diagram 1).

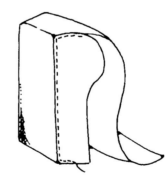

Diagram 1

Repeat to join second 26" edge of back and second back side. Turn. Stuff firmly. Fold ends of back to inside and slipstitch opening closed.

3. Stitch two arm sides to one arm, using the process in Step 2. Repeat to make two arms.

4. Match back to one edge of seat. Slipstitch pieces together on bottom edges (Diagram 2). Place arms on sides. Slipstitch pieces together on bottom edges (Diagram 3).

Diagram 2

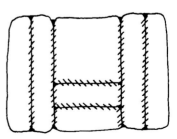

Diagram 3

Using long needle and four long strands of thread, tack through arm below curve to edge of seat, pulling tightly to shape arm and to secure arm to seat. Repeat for opposite arm. Slipstitch front and back of each arm to chair.

5. To make ruffle, fold both long edges to wrong side and overlap (Diagram 4); press.

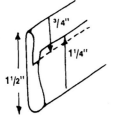

Diagram 4

Cut two 90" pieces of buttonhole twist. Place on overlap on back of ruffle. Zigzag over buttonhole twist through all layers. Gather ruffle by pulling buttonhole twist. Disperse fullness evenly, allowing for ¼" overlap of ends in back. Align bottom edges of ruffle and chair; glue.

Before cutting any fabric, read the General Instructions, page 138.

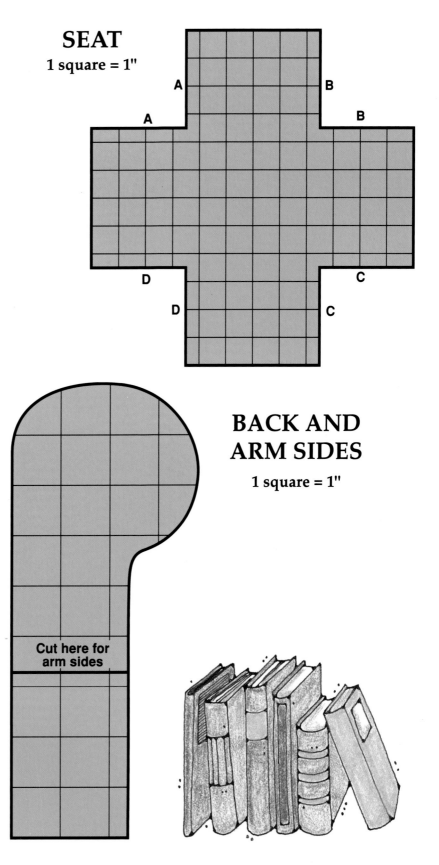

SEAT
1 square = 1"

A   B
A   B
D   C
D   C

BACK AND ARM SIDES

1 square = 1"

Cut here for arm sides

Little Girl Doll

Oh, Romeo, Romeo

FABRICS

★ ¼ yard of white satin:
   Two bodice fronts*
   Four bodice backs*
   Two sleeves*
   One 3" x 5½"
     headdress
★ ⅜ yard of peach crepe:
   Two pinafore fronts
   Four pinafore backs
   One 10" x 45" skirt
★ ¾ yard of peach
   sheer polyester:
   One 24"-wide circle
★ ¾ yard of peach tricot:
   One 25"-wide circle
   One 25"-wide half
     circle for headdress

*Patterns on pages 95 and 96.

MATERIALS

★ ⅝ yard of ⅛"-wide
   elastic
★ Six orange ribbon
   flowers
★ Five white ribbon
   flowers
★ 4¼ yards of ¼"-wide
   light green silk ribbon
★ 3½ yards of ¼"-wide
   apricot silk ribbon
★ Closures
★ Matching thread

DIRECTIONS

1. Stitch one bodice front to two bodice backs at shoulders. Repeat with remaining bodice front and bodice backs. Place right sides of two bodices together, matching shoulder seams. Stitch along one center back seam, around neck and along second center back. Clip curved seam allowances of neck. Turn. Proceed to handle both layers of fabric as one.

2. Repeat Step 1 with pinafore fronts and backs. Place pinafore over bodice, matching shoulder seams and armholes; pin. Proceed to handle both of the pieces as one.

3. Stitch narrow hem in wrist edge of one sleeve. Cut elastic into six equal pieces. On wrong side of sleeve, mark ¾" above and parallel to wrist. Also mark ½" either side of elbow. Stitch one piece of elastic to each mark. Stitch gathering threads along sleeve cap; gather to fit armhole. Stitch sleeve cap to bodice, securing pinafore in seam. Repeat.

4. Stitch side seam from bottom of bodice to hem of sleeve, adjusting all elastic to fit doll and securing it in seam. Repeat.

5. Cut a 5"-wide circle from the center of the polyester circle. Also cut from the outside edge to the center circle. Then round

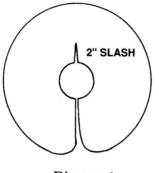

Diagram 1

corners of cut edge (Diagram 1). (The cut edge is the center front of the skirt.) Stitch a rolled hem on the center front and outside edges. Repeat with the tricot circle.

6. Place tricot and polyester circles with right sides together. Cut 2" slash in center back through both layers (Diagram 2). Stitch edges of opening with narrow seam. Clip point. Turn. Match edges of inside circle. Stitch gathering threads around circle. Place center front edges of both circles ¾" from either side of bodice center front. Stitch to bodice.

5" WIDE

Diagram 2

7. Fold skirt with right sides together and short ends matching. Stitch short ends to within 2" of top edge; backstitch. (This seam is the center back; the long edge with the opening is the waist.) Fold edges of opening double to wrong side and stitch with a narrow hem.

8. Stitch gathering threads along waist edge of skirt. Stitch rolled hem in opposite long edge. Match center fronts and gather skirt to fit bodice; stitch. Zigzag over the raw edges of seam allowances at waist. Attach the closures.

9. Attach three white and two orange flowers to center front bodice at waist. Add light green loops for leaves close together behind flowers. Cut three green and five apricot 12" pieces of ribbon. Curl and tack between flowers.

HEADDRESS

10. Stitch rolled hem in curved edge of tricot half-circle. Stitch gathering threads in straight edge. Fold polyester headdress piece with right sides together, matching long edges. Stitch ends. Turn. Matching centers, gather tricot to fit long edge of headdress; stitch. Zigzag all seam allowances.

11. Sew running stitch through each end of satin headdress piece. Gather tightly; secure thread. Decorate each side of headdress, using two orange flowers, one white flower, light green ribbon leaves, three apricot ribbons and three light green ribbons for each side; see Step 9. Attach ribbon scrap to gathered ends of headdress. Tie tightly at center back beneath hair.

Before cutting any fabric, read the General Instructions, page 138.

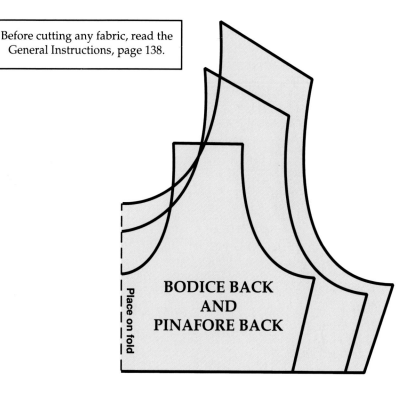

BODICE BACK AND PINAFORE BACK

Place on fold

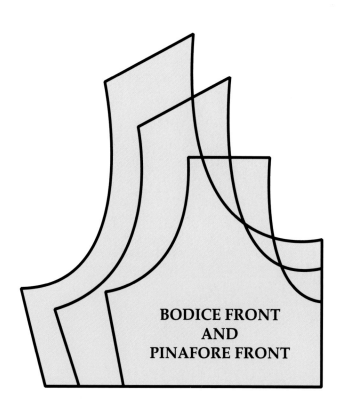

BODICE FRONT AND PINAFORE FRONT

Little Girl Doll

Wedding Bells & Bouquets

DIRECTIONS

1. Cut one 18" x 45" skirt from satin. Fold, matching short ends. Cut a "V" in the center front waist; see pattern. Cut hemline of skirt (Diagram 1). With short ends matching, stitch to within 2" of top edge; backstitch. (This seam is the center back, the long edge with the opening is the waist.) Fold edges of opening double to the wrong side and stitch with a narrow hem.

2. Fold the satin skirt in half, matching center front and back. Trace a pattern for the front and for the back from the satin skirt, placing seams on each side. Cut one skirt front and one skirt back from lace fabric. Stitch sides together. Set aside skirts.

3. Place lace bodice pieces over right side of one set of matching satin pieces. Proceed to handle both layers of fabric as one. Stitch bodice front with lace to two bodice backs with lace at shoulders. Repeat with remaining bodice front

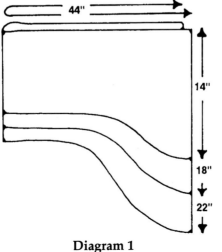

44"

14"

18"

22"

Diagram 1

and bodice backs. Place right sides of two bodices together, matching shoulder seams. Stitch along one center back seam, around neck and along second center back. Clip curved seam allowance of neck. Turn. Proceed to handle all layers of fabric as one. Cut a 6" piece from flat lace. Topstitch lace to neck of dress. Fold down.

4. Place lace sleeves over right side of matching satin sleeves. Proceed to handle as one. Repeat with lace cuffs and satin cuffs. Stitch two cuffs together on edge with point. Clip point. Turn. Stitch gathering threads along sleeve cap and on opposite straight edge. Gather sleeve cap to

fit armhole. Stitch sleeve cap to bodice. Repeat.

5. Stitch side seam from bottom of bodice to hem of sleeve through cuff. Repeat.

6. Cut one 95" piece of cream lace; stitch to edge of lace skirt. Stitch narrow hem in satin skirt. Place lace skirt over right side of satin skirt, matching even edges and center front. Cut slit in center back of lace skirt to align with opening in satin skirt. Stitch gathering threads along waist. Match center fronts and gather skirt to fit bodice; stitch, watching gathers at point in center front to keep smooth. Zigzag over raw edges of seam allowances at waistline. Attach all closures.

7. To make veil, stitch remaining flat lace around edge of tulle circle. Then, fold circle with one-third on top. Place tulle strip between layers of circle with straight edge centered against fold. Stitch gathering threads through all layers close to fold. Gather tightly to fit doll head. Stitch over gathers to secure. Cut two 22" lengths of pearls. Fold one length into two deep loops and tack to one edge of gathers. Repeat. Tack flower sprays to front of gathered edge.

8. Cut one 18" length of pearls and tack to neck of dress, making three loops on one shoulder. Tack the remaining pearls around waist, folding excess into loops at the center front.

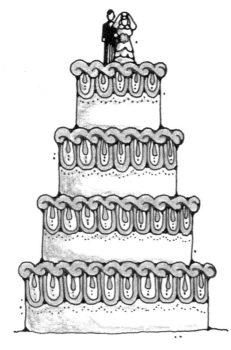

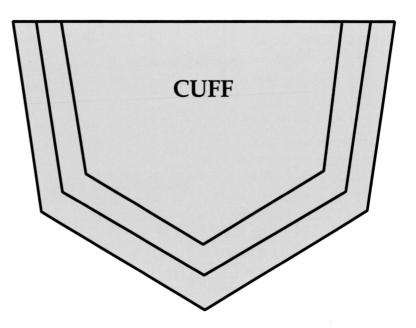

CUFF

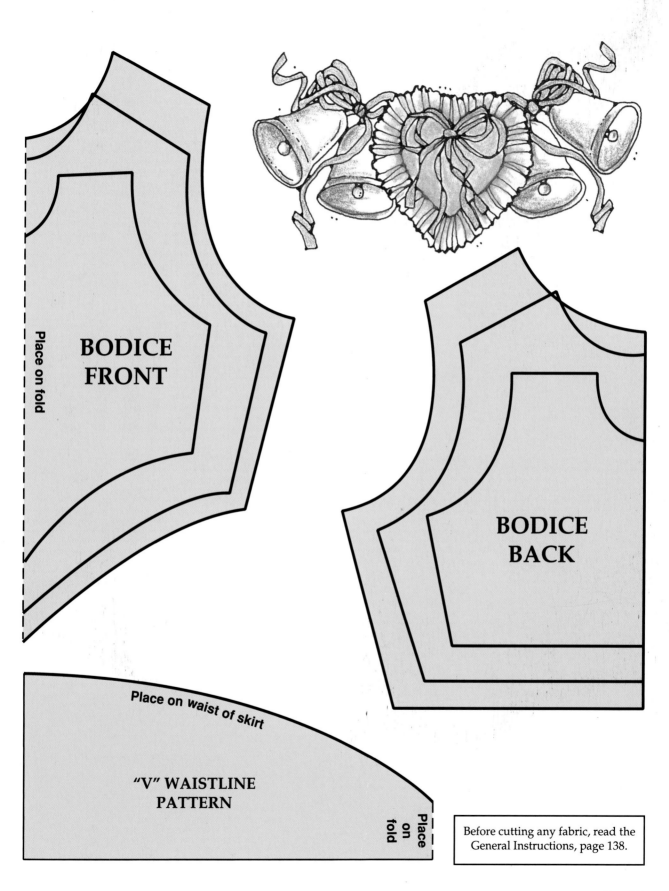

BODICE
FRONT

Place on fold

BODICE
BACK

Place on waist of skirt

"V" WAISTLINE
PATTERN

Place
on
fold

Before cutting any fabric, read the
General Instructions, page 138.

Little Girl Doll

Croquet, Anyone?

FABRIC

★ ½ yard of pink satin:
Two bodice fronts*
Four bodice backs*
Two sleeves*
Two belts
Five skirt panels
One 2¼" x 72" ruffle
Two hat brims;
  see Step 8
One crown; see Step 8

*Patterns on pages 95 and 96.

MATERIALS

★ 7 yards of 2½"-wide
flat white lace
★ Seven dozen ribbon
flowers in the
following colors: light
blue, light pink,
mauve and white
★ 2½ yards of strung
pearls (available with
bridal supplies)

★ 2½ yards of strung
teardrop pearls
(available with bridal
supplies)
★ Small pink, green and
white heart-shaped
buttons
★ 6" of ⅛"-wide elastic
★ Closures
★ Matching threads

DIRECTIONS

DRESS

1. Stitch one bodice front to two bodice backs at shoulders. Repeat with remaining bodice front and bodice backs. Place right sides of two bodices together, matching shoulder seams. Stitch along one center back seam, around neck and along second center back. Clip curved seam allowances of neck. Turn. Proceed to handle both layers of fabric as one.

2. Cut two 26" pieces of lace. Trim one piece 2" from decorative edge. Overlap unfinished edges, placing decorative edges on outside. Zigzag edges together. Fold

on seam. Stitch gathering threads on fold. Gather lace to fit neck. Topstitch to neck of dress.

3. Cut two 23" pieces of lace. Stitch one piece to long edge of one sleeve. Cut elastic in half. Stitch elastic to seam of sleeve/lace. Stitch gathering threads along sleeve cap; gather to fit armhole. Stitch sleeve cap to bodice. Repeat.

4. Stitch side seam from bottom of bodice to wrist of sleeve (lace), adjusting elastic to fit doll and securing it in seam. Repeat.

5. Stitch skirt panels together on long edges, stitching last edge to within 2" of waist edge. Press seams open. (This seam is the center back; the edge with the opening is the waist.) Fold edges of opening double to wrong side and stitch with narrow hem.

6. Stitch narrow hem on one edge of ruffle. Cut one 72" piece of lace. Place lace over ruffle, matching long unfinished edges. Stitch gathering threads through both layers on long raw edge. Matching centers, gather ruffle to fit bottom edge of skirt; stitch. Attach the closures.

7. Stitch two belts together, leaving an opening. Clip the corners. Turn. Slipstitch the opening closed. Attach one closure.

8. Attach ribbon flowers and pearls to center front of belt and to neck between layers of lace ruffles. Tack matching ribbon flowers to each sleeve. Add buttons as desired.

Before cutting any fabric, read the General Instructions, page 138.

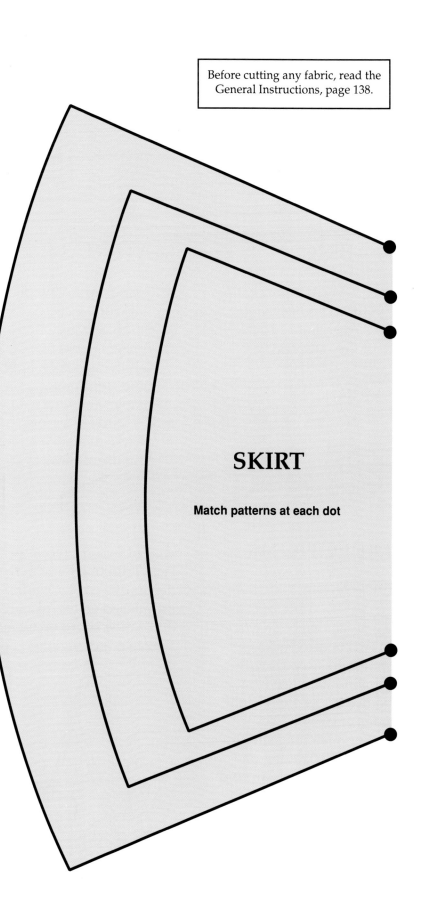

SKIRT

Match patterns at each dot

HAT

9. Trace outside edge of hat brim. Measure inside opening. Make circle in center the size of the opening. Cut two hat brims, to inside and ¼" to outside edges. Measure width of crown of hat from one brim to the other. Cut one crown, adding ½" seam allowance.

Center and glue crown over hat. Stitch brims together on outside edges. Turn. Slide over hat brim. Slipstitch top inside edge of brim to crown. Clip seam allowance on bottom inside edge of brim; glue seam allowance to inside of hat. Cut two 60" pieces of lace. Stitch gathering threads in unfinished edge of one

piece. Gather lace to fit bottom of brim; glue. Repeat with lace on top of hat brim.

10. Stitch or glue ribbon flowers to hat. Then drape and tack the pearls as desired. Repeat on seam above ruffle.

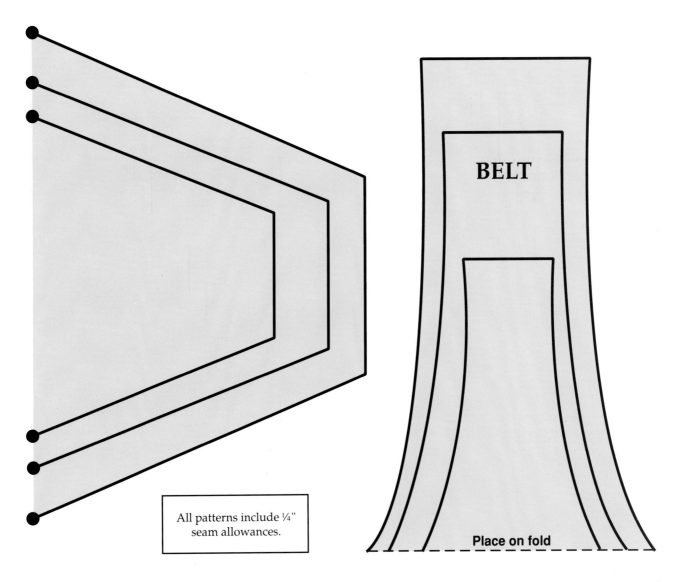

All patterns include ¼" seam allowances.

BELT

Place on fold

Little Girl Doll

Harvest Princess

DIRECTIONS

1. Complete Steps 1 through 5 of Basic Little Girl Doll Dress.

2. Sponge paint suede, using apricot the most, gold and rust the least. Cut 120 large leaves and twenty small leaves, using pinking shears. Paint dark green veins in leaves.

3. Beginning ½" to ¾" above hem of dress, tack one row of large leaves around bottom of dress, overlapping leaves. Continue to tack leaves in rows to cover most of skirt.

4. Tack one end of small leaves to neck of dress, overlapping leaves.

5. Tie ribbon into bow around waist. Cut one spray of berries apart. Wrap spray around waist, twisting spray at back to secure. Wrap second spray into a wreath to make headdress.

LARGE LEAF

SMALL LEAF

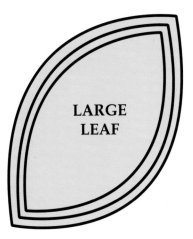

Little Girl Doll

Masquerade Mystic

FABRICS	MATERIALS
★ ½ yard of copper lame': Two sleeves* Four overskirts One bodice overlay One 1½" x 9" ruffle (cut on bias) Two 2" x 3" masks (cut on bias) ★ ¼ yard of black/copper: Two bodice fronts* Four bodice backs* Two cuffs* One 9" x 27" skirt ★ ¼ yard fusible knit interfacing: Two sleeves* Four overskirts One bodice overlay	★ 6 yards of 1¼"-wide gathered white lace ★ Copper metallic spray paint ★ Copper metallic thread ★ 1¼ yards of ⅜"-wide trim ★ Acrylic paints for masks ★ Two flat ceramic masks** ★ One molded ceramic mask** ★ Three blue faceted jewels ★ Four small black feathers ★ One 6" long x ⅛"-wide dowel ★ Glue gun and glue ★ Closures ★ Matching threads
*Patterns on pages 95, 96 and 110.	**See Suppliers

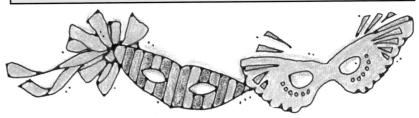

DIRECTIONS

1. Spray paint all trim. Paint flat ceramic masks as desired. Fuse the interfacing to matching fabric pieces, following the manufacturer's instructions.

2. Fold long edges of bodice overlay under ¼". Center and topstitch to right side of one bodice front. Cut one 5" piece of trim. Glue the trim to edges of overlay.

3. Stitch one bodice front to two bodice backs at shoulders. Repeat with remaining bodice front and bodice backs.

4. Fold the ruffle, matching long edges. Fold ¼" inside on each end. Stitch gathering threads on long edges. Gather the ruffle to fit neck; stitch.

5. Place right sides of two bodices together, matching shoulder seams. Stitch along one center back seam, around neck, catching ruffle

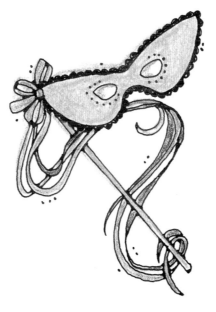

in seam, and along second center back. Clip curved seam allowances of neck. Turn. Proceed to handle both layers of fabric as one.

6. Stitch gathering threads on cap and long straight edge of one sleeve. Gather straight edge of sleeve to fit cuff. Fold one cuff with wrong sides together. Matching centers, stitch long edges to bottom edge of sleeve. Gather sleeve to fit armhole. Stitch sleeve cap to bodice. Repeat.

7. Stitch the side seam from bottom of bodice to edge of cuff.

8. Make ½" deep hem in one long edge of skirt. Cut eight 27" pieces of lace. Stitch first row of lace 1" above and parallel to hem.

Repeat to attach all pieces of lace, placing top row ¼" from top edge of skirt. Spray paint lace until nearly covered. Allow to dry. Fold skirt with right sides together and short ends matching. Stitch short ends to within 2" of top edge; backstitch. (This seam is the center back; the long edge with the opening is the waist.) Fold edges of the opening double to wrong side and stitch with a narrow hem.

9. Stitch two overskirts with right sides together along center back seam to within 2" of the waist edge; backstitch. Repeat with remaining two overskirt pieces. Stitch outside edge of overskirts with right sides together, leaving the waist edge open. Clip curved seam allowances. Turn. Slipstitch seams of center back opening closed. Glue trim to outside edge of the overskirt.

10. Place overskirt over skirt front, matching center back openings and waist edges and placing curved edges of overskirt ⅛" from center mark. Stitch gathering threads on the waist edge through all layers. Gather skirt to fit bodice. Matching center fronts, stitch skirt to bodice. Zigzag over raw edges at waist. Attach the closures.

11. To make mask, color edges of eye holes of molded ceramic mask with marker or paint. Glue back of one fabric mask and place on molded mask front, molding fabric to shape of mask. Trim edges to ¼", then fold to back. Cut a slit in eye hole. Fold fabric inside eye hole; glue. Repeat for back of mask, trimming lame' slightly smaller than ceramic mask. Wrap dowel with copper metallic thread, gluing ends to secure. Using glue gun, glue dowel on back right edge of mask. Glue feathers as desired over dowel. Glue three jewels to the forehead of mask.

12. Cut two 15" pieces of copper metallic thread. Fold one in half and thread through hole in painted mask, making a half-hitch knot. Repeat. Knot two pieces of thread together, varying length of thread. Tie ends around doll waist.

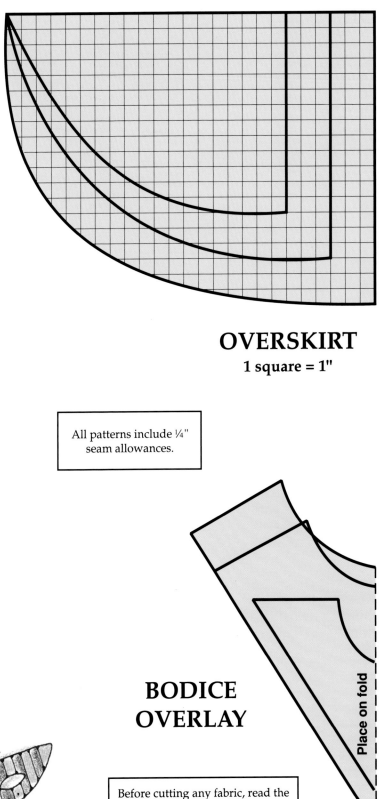

OVERSKIRT
1 square = 1"

All patterns include ¼" seam allowances.

BODICE OVERLAY

Place on fold

Before cutting any fabric, read the General Instructions, page 138.

Little Girl Doll

The Princess and the Pea

FABRICS	MATERIALS
★ ⅝ yard of blue satin: One bodice front* Two bodice backs* Two sleeves* One 7" x 38" skirt One 5½" x 38" skirt Two 2" x 60" ruffles One 2½" x 8" waistband ★ 1 yard of blue sparkle: One bodice front* Two bodice backs* Two short sleeves* Four overskirts	★ 6" to 8" of ⅛"-wide elastic ★ 12" of ¾"-wide flat white lace ★ 3½ yards of 2"-wide flat white lace ★ 2 cups of dried rose buds ★ 2½ yards of pink net ribbon ★ Closures ★ Matching threads

*Patterns on pages 95 and 96.

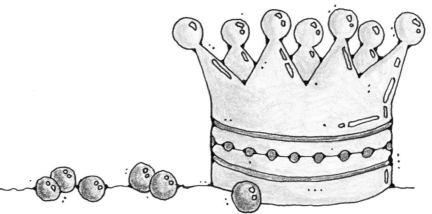

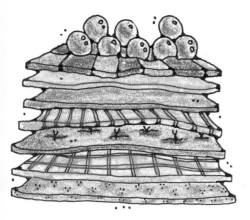

DIRECTIONS

1. Stitch one sparkle bodice front to two bodice backs at shoulders. Repeat with satin bodice front and backs. Stitch gathering threads in straight edge of 12" piece of ¾"-wide lace. Gather to fit bodice neck; stitch. Place right sides of two bodices together, matching shoulder seams. Stitch across back waist, along one center back seam, around neck, along second center back and along second back waist. Clip curved seam allowance of neck. Turn. Carefully fold sides of waist edges, matching but without turning, bodice at neck. Stitch bodice front waist. Clip point. Turn.

2. Stitch narrow hem in wrist edge of one satin sleeve. Cut elastic in half. Stitch one piece of elastic ½" above hem. Fold one short

sleeve in half, matching sleeve caps. Match sleeve caps of short sleeve and satin sleeve. Proceed to handle all layers of fabric as one. Stitch gathering threads along sleeve cap; gather to fit armhole. Stitch sleeve cap to bodice. Repeat. Attach closures.

3. Fold waistband with right sides together, matching long edges. Stitch ends; turn. Set aside.

4. Cut two 60" pieces of 2"-wide lace. Stitch narrow hem in one long edge of one ruffle. Place lace over right side of ruffle, matching long raw edges. Stitch gathering threads through both layers. Gather ruffle to fit one long edge of 7"-wide skirt. Repeat with remaining ruffle, lace and 5½"-wide skirt piece.

5. Fold one skirt with right sides together and short ends matching. Stitch short ends to within 2" of top edge; backstitch. Fold edges of opening double to wrong side and stitch with narrow hem. Repeat with remaining skirt.

6. Match center back edges of two overskirt pieces. Stitch from bottom edge to within 2" of the top edge; backstitch. Repeat with

remaining overskirt pieces. Place overskirts together, matching center backs and all edges. Stitch outside edge of overskirts together. Fill with rose buds. Slip-stitch center backs together. Stitch gathering threads along waist edge.

7. Place wrong side of short satin shirt over right side of long satin skirt, then place overskirt over satin skirts. Stitch gathering threads along raw edges through all layers. Matching centers, gather skirt to fit waistband; stitch. Zigzag over raw edges of seam allowance.

8. Cut two 45" pieces of ribbon net. Mark 2" intervals around skirts on the ruffle seams. Couch about 2½" of ribbon net at each interval. Tie the bow with remaining ribbon net. Tack to the waistband.

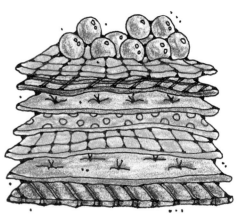

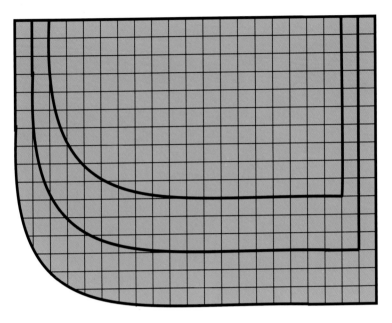

OVERSKIRT
1 square = 1"

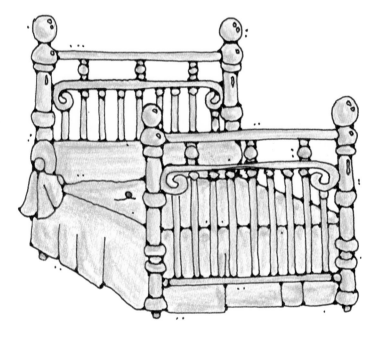

*Hans Christian Andersen, author of **The Princess and the Pea**, wrote many plays, poems and novels. His fame, however, rests on his **Fairy Tales and Stories**, written between 1835 and 1872.*

Andersen was born in the slums of Odense, Denmark, on April 2, 1805. His father, a poor shoemaker, was literate; his mother, however, was uneducated and superstitious. Hans received little formal education, and was hopelessly poor at spelling. His father died in 1816, and, at the age of 14, young Andersen went to Copenhagen with the vague hope of becoming a singer, a dancer, or an actor. After much hardship and many disappointments, he succeeded in becoming associated with the Royal Theater, but he had to leave when his voice began to change.

*Profoundly self-centered, Andersen wrote and rewrote his memoirs, the standard edition of which is generally considered to be **The Fairy Tale of My Life** (1855). Other famous fairy tales written by Hans Andersen include **The Emperor's New Clothes, The Ugly Duckling** and **The Little Mermaid**.*

Little Girl Doll

Ain't She Sweet!

FABRICS

★ ⅝ yard of turquoise lightweight fabric:
  One bodice front
  Two bodice backs
  Two sleeves
  One 3" x 36" skirt
  One 4" x 36" skirt
  One 2½" x 30" tie
  Two 11" x 2" straps
  One 2½" x 25" bow
  One 2" x 6¼" neck
    band (cut on bias)
  Two pantalets*
*Pattern on pages 98 and 99.

MATERIALS

★ ½ yard of ⅛"-wide elastic
★ Closures
★ Matching threads

DIRECTIONS

DRESS

1. Stitch one turquoise bodice front and two turquoise bodice backs at shoulders. Stitch narrow hem in wrist edge of sleeve. Repeat. Sew elastic to wrong side of one sleeve 1" from wrist edge. Gather to 1½". Stitch gathering threads in the sleeve cap; repeat. Match center of sleeve cap to one shoulder seam. Gather sleeve to fit armhole. Stitch sleeve to bodice. Repeat. Fold bodice with right sides together. Stitch side seam from bottom of bodice to hem of sleeve, adjusting elastic to fit doll and securing it in the seam. Repeat.

2. Center and stitch neck band to neck with right sides together and using ½" seam. Fold ends inside. Then fold 1" to wrong side. Turn under raw edge ½" and slipstitch.

3. Fold one strap to measure 1" wide. Stitch long edge. Turn. Repeat. Center strap on shoulder seam; tack. Pin ends to bottom edge of bodice.

4. Stitch short ends of one turquoise skirt together. Repeat. Stitch narrow hem on one long edge of both pieces. Place long piece under short skirt, matching seams and with right sides up. (The seams are the center backs.) Stitch gathering threads along raw edges through both layers. Matching centers, gather skirts to fit bodice; stitch, securing strap ends.

5. Mark each strap ¾" above seam joining skirt and bodice. Topstitch a horizontal line; backstitch. Repeat. Attach closures.

6. Fold tie to measure 1¼" wide. Trim ends at 45-degree angle. Stitch ends and long sides, leaving an opening. Trim corners. Turn. Slipstitch opening closed. Insert belt under straps in loops.

7. Trim ends of bow at 45-degree angle. Stitch narrow hem on all edges. Tie into bow and pin in doll's hair.

PANTALETS

8. With right sides of pantalets together, stitch center front and center back seams. Then stitch inseam.

9. Make ½" casing at waist. Measure waist of doll. Cut piece of elastic same as measurement. Insert and overlap ends ½" and secure. Slipstitch opening closed. Stitch a narrow hem in each leg. Sew elastic ½" above each hemmed edge. Gather to fit the doll and secure.

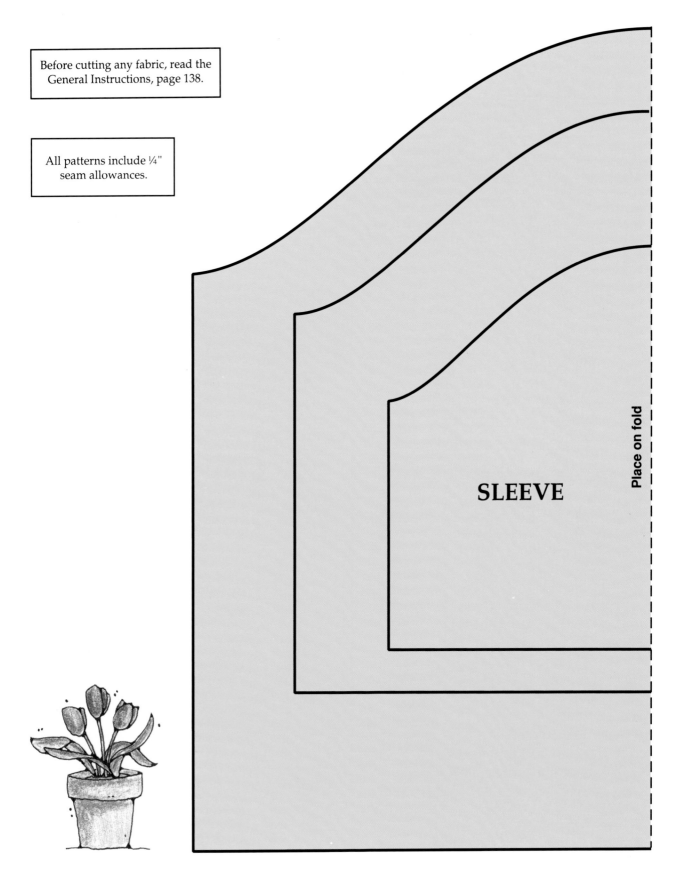

Before cutting any fabric, read the General Instructions, page 138.

All patterns include ¼" seam allowances.

SLEEVE

Place on fold

HANDBAG

★ 75 yards of 2-ply lame'
  silver thread
★ Crochet hook No. 10

Note: Beg ch or chs counts
as one st.

Ch 22.

   Rnd 1: Dc in 4th ch from
hook and in ea rem ch = 20
dc, work around in other
side of foundation ch, dc in
next 20 sts, sl st to top of
beg st. Crease along
foundation ch to form a
pocket.

   Work in back lp only for
Rnds. 2-6.

   Rnd 2: Ch 4, (sk next dc,
dc in next dc, ch 1) around
end, sl st to 3rd ch of beg
ch-4.

   Rnd 3: Ch 3, dc in ea dc
and ea ch around sl st to top
of beg ch 3 = 40 dc.

   Rnd 4: Rep Rnd 2.
   Rnd 5: Rep Rnd 3.
   Rnd 6: Rep Rnd 2.
   Rnd 7: Work through
both lps (Ch 3, 2 dc in same
st as sl st, sk next 3 sts, sl st
in next st) across, end, sl st
in same st as beg sl st, do
not fasten off.

   Carry strap: (Ch 3, dc in
3rd ch from hook) 12 times,
sc to opposite side of bag.
Fasten off.

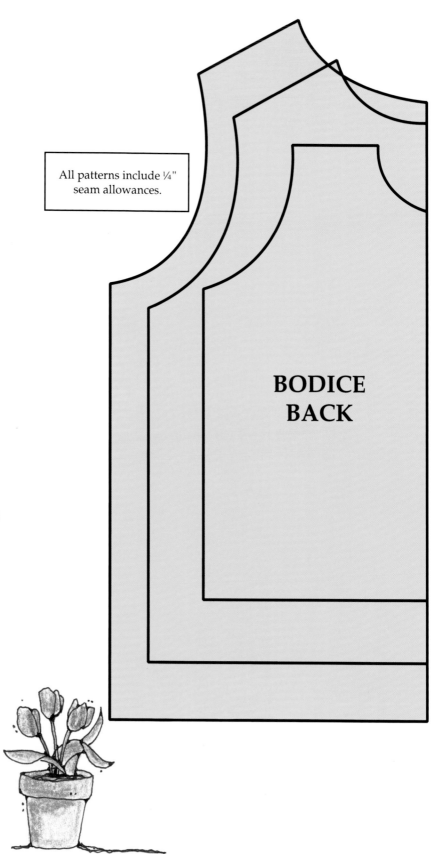

All patterns include ¼"
seam allowances.

**BODICE
BACK**

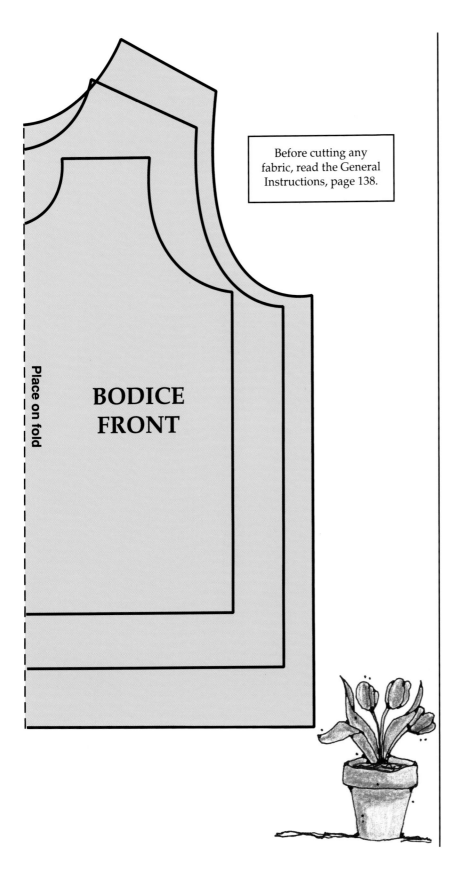

Place on fold

**BODICE
FRONT**

Before cutting any fabric, read the General Instructions, page 138.

DID YOU KNOW. . .

One of the most drastic revolutions to hit the fashion world came with the "Roaring '20s." Everything changed. The hair was cut in mannish style, the figure flattened to a sexless silhouette, and the waistline and hemline almost met—the drop waisted dress was born.

The teenager began asserting herself as a result of the greater freedom for women. This period, too, saw the introduction of man-made synthetic fibers, and attention was given to molding the figure rather than confining it.

Adults and children, heavy and slender, all wore the same styles, whether they were becoming or not. All sorts of make-up were worn. True, outfits were designed specifically for every activity of milady, but all along the same basic pattern.

Since the flapper first declared her independence, more attention has been paid to fashions for the young. For countless centuries, children were simply miniature adults—whereas during the past fifty years, all this has changed and there are specialists designing for the different age groups.

Little Girl Doll

Puss 'n' Boots

FABRICS

★ ⅛ yard of aqua
lightweight fabric:
Four shirt fronts
Two shirt backs
Two collars
Two sleeves
Two hat brims;
  see Step 7
One crown;
  see Step 7
One ½" x 4" hatband
★ ¼ yard of apricot print:
Four vest fronts
Two vest backs
Four knickers
One 2" x 6" waistband
Two 1½" x 3"
  leg bands

MATERIALS

★ One 4¼"-wide
mesh hat
★ Four 4"-long apricot
feathers
★ ¾ yard of ¼"-wide
aqua satin ribbon
★ Seven aqua beads
★ 6" of ⅛"-wide elastic
★ Flat black paint or
purchased boots
★ Three closures
★ Matching threads

DIRECTIONS

SHIRT

1. Stitch one shirt front to two shirt backs at shoulders. Repeat with remaining shirt front and shirt backs. Place right sides of collars together; stitch, leaving inside edge open.

Clip curved seam allowances. Turn. Baste collar to right side of shirt at neck. Place right sides of two shirts together with collar between, matching shoulder seams. Stitch along one center front, around neck, securing collar, and second center front. Clip curved seam allowances. Turn.

Proceed to handle both layers of fabric as one.

2. Stitch narrow hem in wrist edge of one sleeve. Cut elastic in half. Stitch one piece of elastic ½" above hem. Stitch gathering threads along sleeve cap; gather to fit armhole. Stitch sleeve cap to shirt. Repeat.

3. Stitch side seam from bottom of shirt to hem of sleeve, adjusting elastic to fit doll and securing it in seam. Repeat. Attach two closures inside front opening. Sew aqua beads to front, evenly spaced along front opening.

VEST

4. Stitch one vest back to two vest fronts at shoulder and side seams. Repeat with remaining vest fronts and vest back. Place right sides of two vests together, matching shoulder seams. Stitch outer edge of vests, leaving an opening in bottom back edge. Clip curved seam allowances. Turn. Slipstitch opening closed. Fold seam allowance of armhole to inside, clipping as needed; slipstitch. Repeat.

KNICKERS

5. Stitch two knickers together. Stitch gathering threads along bottom edge. Gather to fit one leg band.

Fold band, matching long edges and with wrong sides together. Stitch band to bottom edge of knickers. Stitch leg inseam. Repeat. Put one leg inside the other with right sides together. Stitch center seam to within 1" of waist edge on back (Diagram 1).

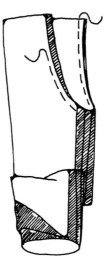

Diagram 1

6. Fold the waistband with right sides together and long edges matching. Stitch short ends. Turn. Stitch gathering threads along waist of knickers. Match the centers and gather waist to fit waistband; stitch. Attach closure.

HAT

7. Trace outside edge of hat brim. Measure inside opening. Make circle in center the size of the opening. Cut two hat brims, adding ¼" seam allowance to inside and outside edges. Measure width of crown from one brim to the other. Cut one crown, adding ½" seam allownce. Center and glue crown over hat. Stitch brims together on outside edges. Turn. Slide over hat brim. Slipstitch top inside edge of brim to crown. Clip

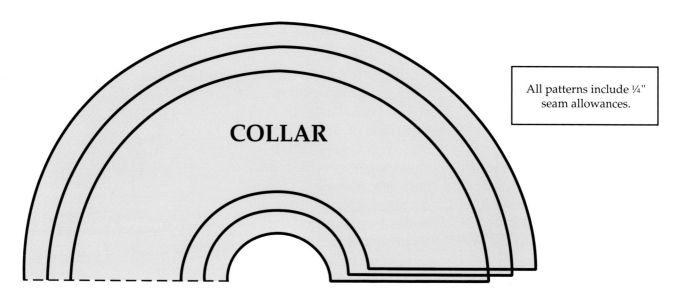

COLLAR

All patterns include ¼" seam allowances.

seam allowance on bottom inside edge of brim. Glue seam allowance to inside of hat.

8. Twist hatband and glue to inner top of rim. Glue feathers to top of hat.

Before cutting any fabric, read the General Instructions, page 138.

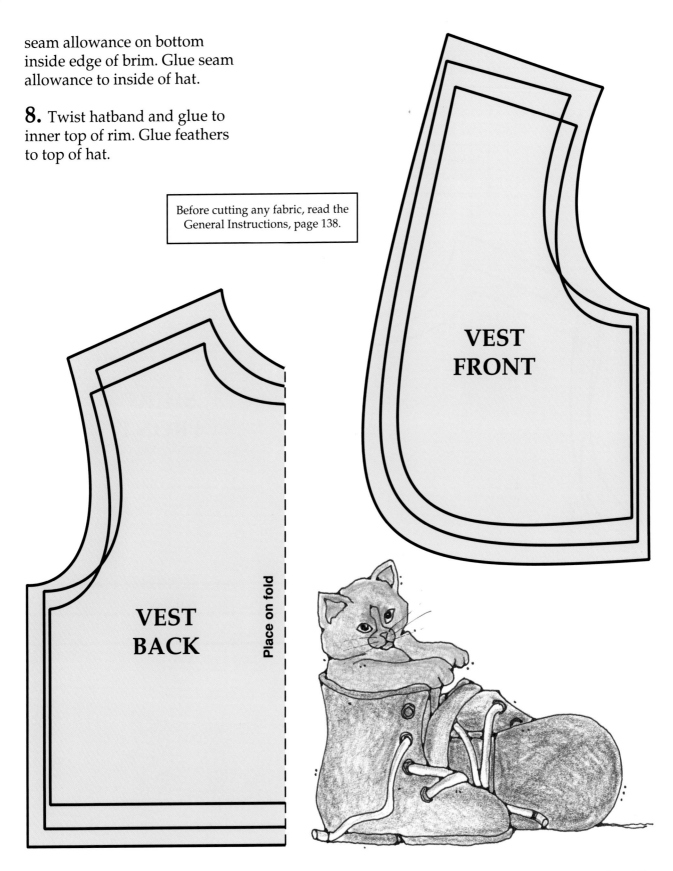

VEST FRONT

VEST BACK

Place on fold

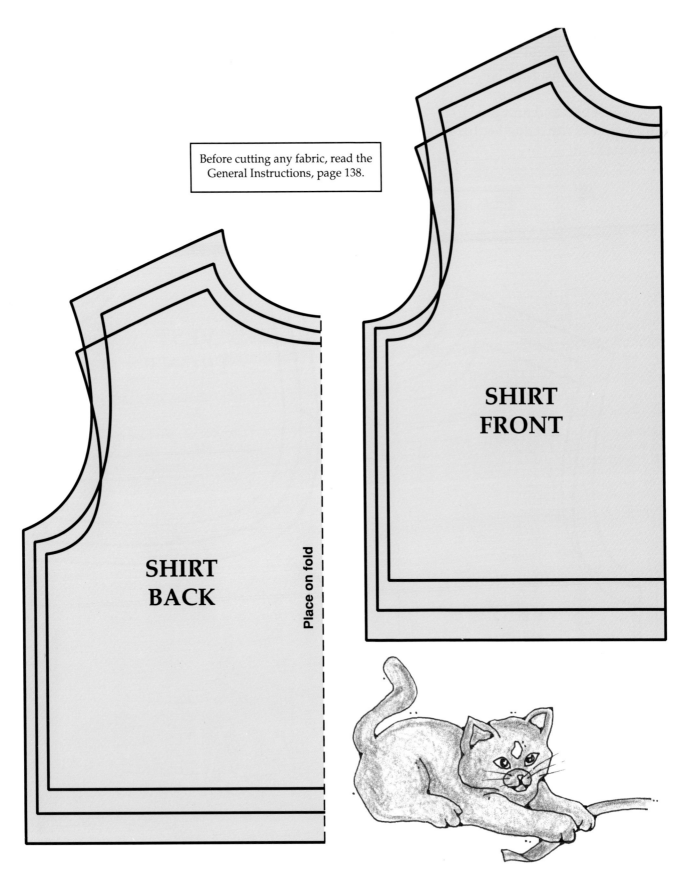

Before cutting any fabric, read the
General Instructions, page 138.

**SHIRT
FRONT**

**SHIRT
BACK**

Place on fold

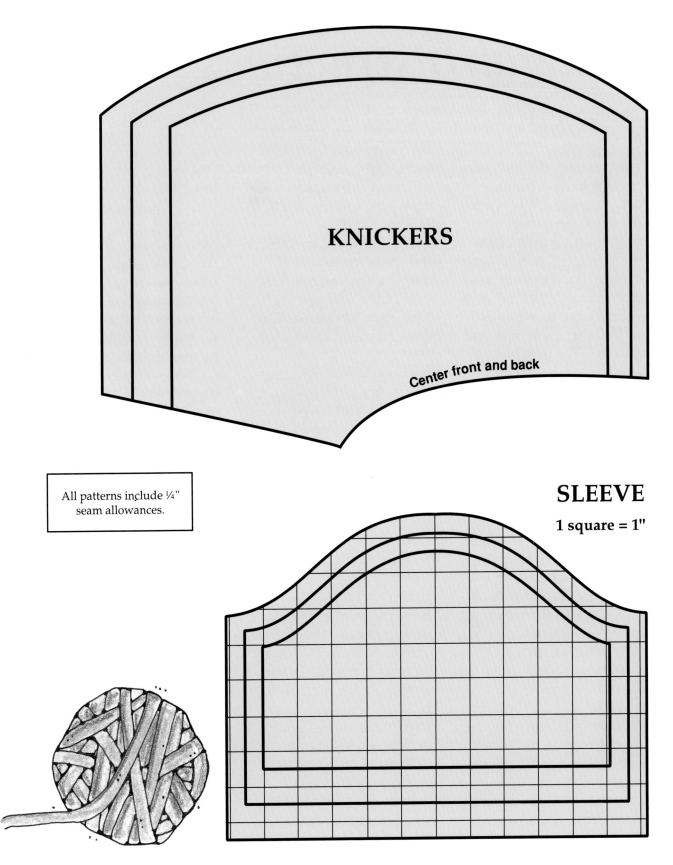

KNICKERS

Center front and back

All patterns include ¼"
seam allowances.

SLEEVE

1 square = 1"

General Instructions

IT'S FUN!

Dolls, just like the girls who are their human counterparts, come in many shapes and sizes. As a consequence, fitting their clothing can be just as exacting a process! Baby dolls typically have a fat tummy and a round bottom, while little girl dolls are more lean and willowy. The teen fashion dolls have exaggerated waistlines and bosoms. A jointed doll adds another set of variables. Thus, some general guidelines for fitting doll clothes will be helpful.

First and foremost, always make doll clothing with your doll close at hand for frequent and accurate fittings. In some cases, you may find it easier to attach trims to the doll once she is dressed. Dolls have fewer joints than real girls and additional space must be allowed. Armholes, in particular, need to be large. Some dolls have narrow or non-existent shoulders and the fitting of the clothing needs to allow for that. Thus, the fit-as-you-stitch plan assures the most success.

Second, some doll clothing must allow for movement. Baby dolls that sit will need extra space in the hip width and leg length to fit attractively.

As you select the fabrics and trims for your doll clothing, keep in mind the scale of the doll you are dressing. Fabric selection alone has been known to "make or break" a doll clothing project. The best choices are tightly woven, medium weight fabrics. Lightweight or coarsely woven fabrics are workable if interfaced with a lightweight, fusible interfacing. In addition to the fabric, select carefully the buttons, trims, ribbons and lace to fit the scale of the doll herself. Consider the possibilities of cutting a trim in half or using the wrong side of a print to achieve the look you want. Even bias bindings and hems need to be narrow. In keeping with the scale, some products may substitute nicely for another, such as beads for buttons, an ornament for jewelry, or vice versa.

In every case, the directions for making these doll clothes include procedures that will make your task as easy as possible. For example, it is easier to fully line the bodice of a dress than to make a small facing. Similarly, cuffs are sewn onto sleeves before closing the sleeve seam. In some cases, you may choose to hem a dress by hand, even though the model in the photo was done by machine.

You will also want to determine the expected use of your doll. A doll that is going to be dressed and undressed by young hands must be sturdy and durable. A doll for display can be more intricately trimmed and decorated, and may only need to be slipstitched closed in the back.

While we recognize the impossibility of such a thought, we would like to see the dolls you are dressing and to talk with you about each variation in detail. Like you, we know that dolls can be as delightful to dress as real girls.

VOCABULARY

★ **Baste.** Basting stitches are temporary stitches done by hand or machine to hold layers of fabric in place. Remove basting stitches once the process is complete.

★ **Bias.** Fabric, when cut at a 45-degree angle to its grain, is cut on the bias. The term often refers to pieces cut in strips and sewn together for the purpose of binding a raw edge.

★ **Binding.** Bias cuts of the fabric are ordinarily used for binding, although it is not essential. The bias and clothing are stitched with right sides together. Then the opposite raw edge of the bias is folded under, usually ¼". That edge is folded to the back and the first fold is stitched, either by machine or hand.

★ **Bodice.** The portion of the dress which is above the waist, including the sleeves, is the bodice.

★ **Casing.** A casing is created to house elastic, frequently in the waist of clothing. It must be wide enough to allow the elastic to move smoothly inside. To make a casing for ¼"- wide elastic, for example,

first fold a ¼" seam allowance to the wrong side of the fabric. Then fold again ½", also to the wrong side. Stitch close to the first fold through all layers, leaving an opening. Insert elastic, overlap ends ½" and secure. Stitch opening closed.

★ **Clip.** Clipping is the process of cutting a short slit in the seam allowance of the fabric that is perpendicular to the seam to allow easement of bulk. Clipping curves is usually a diagonal cut in the seam allowance. The excess is discarded, thereby reducing the bulk once the piece is right-side-out.

★ **Closures.** Closures on doll clothing are determined primarily by the way the clothing is to be use. Small snaps, either plastic or metal are good for closures. Buttons and button-holes always add reality to doll clothing. For clothing a child is going to use, hook and loop tape is easy to attach. Most doll clothes need only half the width of a ¾"-wide strip. The disadvantage is that the tape is bulky and the stitching shows on the right side of the clothing.

★ **Couch.** Couching stitches are decorative as

well as practical. They are used to anchor a laid product, such as a length of ribbon, by stitching over it, thereby attaching it to the fabric.

★ **Dressmakers' pen.** This tool, available in the notions department of fabric stores, is either water soluble or air soluble. In some cases in this book, it is called for specifically in order to make a temporary mark on the fabric. It is generally useful in all sewing, however.

★ **Elastic** (to attach). Place the piece of elastic on the wrong side of the fabric with one end matching the raw edge. Machine tack stitch elastic to fabric and, without cutting the thread, set the machine for a wide, loose zigzag stitch. Zigzag over the elastic, not catching any elastic in the stitches. Proceed to work with the piece as directed. Then, before stitching the seam to secure the elastic, pull it to gather the fabric.

★ **Enlarging patterns.** Patterns that are too large for the pages of the book are prepared on a grid in which each square is equal to 1" on the finished pattern. To enlarge a pattern, select a piece of paper large enough to accommodate the finished size of the pattern. Mark grid lines 1" apart to fill the pattern. Begin marking dots on the corresponding grid lines. Connect the dots. A product made for this purpose is available in fabric stores. It has dots printed on it at 1" intervals. One-inch graph paper can also be used.

★ **Fold double.** To turn under the raw edge and then to fold it again, completely covering it, is to fold double.

★ **Gathers.** Gathering threads are two rows of long, loose machine stitches sewn on the right side of the fabric ¼" and ½" from and parallel to the cut edge of the fabric. To gather, anchor threads on one end by wrapping in figure-eight around straight pin. Hold threads on opposite end and push fabric into small folds. In most cases, disperse the fullness evenly. To secure the gathers, stitch on the seam line with a regular length stitch. Always remove all gathering threads.

★ **Motif.** A single design, usually repeated in a pattern, is a motif. It is common in lace and trim and you may need to adjust measurements to place a motif as you desire, such as in the center.

★ **Narrow hem.** A narrow hem is the smallest distance that can be folded double to the wrong side and stitched. In each case, the bulk and width vary according to the fabric being used. Some machines have attachments and special stitches that make narrow hems easier and more attractive.

★ **Notches.** Some pattern pieces are marked with small notches. Match the notched edges to align pieces correctly.

★ **Paint** (mixing). The paints called for in this book are acrylic and are available from several manufacturers and in many colors. It still may be necessary to mix colors to get the desired shade. Always mix enough of a color to complete a project; it is very difficult to match a color later. Acrylic paint as it comes in the container is a good consistency for stencilling. Add only a few drops of water, if any.

★ **Patterns.** To make patterns from the pages of this book, use tracing paper. Transfer all information such as "place on fold." All patterns include ¼" seam allowance. Patterns are not provided for circles, rectangles or squares. In such cases, measurements are given. You may wish to make your own patterns for these. See "Alterations" before cutting any pieces.

★ **Raw edge.** The unfinished edge, usually cut with scissors, is sometimes called a raw edge.

★ **Ribbon flowers.** Although ribbon flowers can be made by hand, all of them used on the models in this book are purchased. They are available in the notions department and may come by the yard or in small packages. In some cases the leaves have been removed and replaced with loops of ribbon to match the trim on the dress.

★ **Rolled hem.** Similar to a narrow hem, the rolled hem calls for an attachment on the sewing machine which turns under about ⅛" of fabric twice and holds it in place while being stitched.

★ **Running stitch.** Running stitches are small, evenly spaced stitches sewn by hand. They may be used to gather fabric.

★ **Seam allowance.** The space between the stitched seam and the raw edge of the fabric. All patterns and measurements in this book include a ¼" seam allowance except where noted in specific cases. Seam allowances of curved seams should be clipped to create ease. Corner seam allowances should be trimmed to reduce bulk.

★ **Sleeve cap.** The top of the sleeve which is nearest the shoulder. It may be flat or gathered and is sewn into the armhole, usually after the bodice front and back are constructed.

★ **Slipstitch.** Small, inconspicuous stitches taken by hand to secure a seam. They are usually worked in one strand of matching thread.

★ **Stencilling.** Stencilling is a method of painting a pattern onto a surface by using a thin sheet in which the design has been cut out. Cut the template from clear plastic sheets (available in craft stores for that purpose) or from manila folders. Use a craft knife to cut the stencil, trying to make long, smooth cuts. Pin or tape the fabric to a flat surface. Then pin or tape the stencil to the fabric. Use small amounts of paint and a nearly dry brush. Dab the paint in a stippling motion, first to edges, then to the center of the design.

★ **Tack.** To tack fabric or trim is to join two or more layers with small, inconspicuous hand stitches.

★ **Topstitch.** Topstitching is done on the right side of the fabric by machine. Usually it follows the seam line and adds a decorative touch.

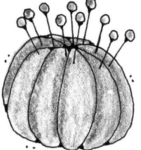

ALTERATIONS

Every consideration has been given to careful and accurate measurements in this book. It is impossible, however, to allow for the wide variations which occur between doll bodies.

Yardages and measurements in the directions are given for the middle-sized baby doll and little girl doll and for the large fashion doll. Knowing that, you may need to buy additional fabric or trim, even one more button. You should always work with your doll close at hand and measure before cutting any pieces, especially waistbands, cuffs, elastic or rectangular skirt pieces.

For minor alterations, make the following measurements on your doll using a tape measure:

a. from shoulder to waist over fullest part of chest.
b. from underarm to underarm over fullest part of chest.
c. from shoulder to waist in back.
d. from underarm to underarm across back.

Trace the pattern and compare measurements with pattern itself, making adjustments for seam allowances and providing ½" to ¾" give.

If the pattern needs to be increased, cut it into halves or quarters, as needed, and place it over another piece

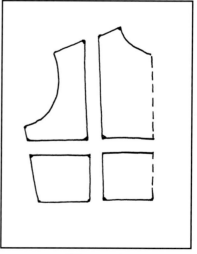

Diagram 1

of tissue paper (Diagram 1). Depending upon the measurements, your pattern pieces may no longer be parallel to each other (Diagram 2).

If the pattern needs to be made smaller, cut it into halves or quarters, as needed, and overlap to the correct size; tape together. It may not be necessary to redraw.

Using the same principles for minor alterations, sleeves and pants may also be changed. The horizontal cuts should be under the

curved edges (Diagrams 3 and 4).

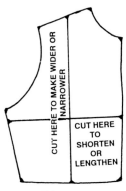

Diagram 4

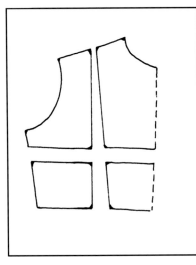

Diagram 2

Keep the center front and center back straight, however. Check the new waist measurement, adjusting for seam allowances. Redraw the pattern.

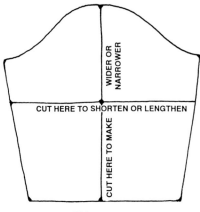

Diagram 3

Even if the pattern appears to fit your doll, here are some areas to check measurements:
- ✓ neckline
- ✓ shoulder width
- ✓ sleeve length
- ✓ wrist
- ✓ waist
- ✓ seat
- ✓ skirt length

Finally, keep your doll close at hand. Remember to fit-as-you-stitch and your doll's clothes will, indeed, be a perfect fit.

METRIC EQUIVALENCY CHART

MM—MILLIMETRES   CM—CENTIMETRES

INCHES TO MILLIMETRES AND CENTIMETRES

INCHES	MM	CM	INCHES	CM	INCHES	CM
⅛	3	0.3	9	22.9	30	76.2
¼	6	0.6	10	25.4	31	78.7
⅜	10	1.0	11	27.9	32	81.3
½	13	1.3	12	30.5	33	83.8
⅝	16	1.6	13	33.0	34	86.4
¾	19	1.9	14	35.6	35	88.9
⅞	22	2.2	15	38.1	36	91.4
1	25	2.5	16	40.6	37	94.0
1¼	32	3.2	17	43.2	38	96.5
1½	38	3.8	18	45.7	39	99.1
1¾	44	4.4	19	48.3	40	101.6
2	51	5.1	20	50.8	41	104.1
2½	64	6.4	21	53.3	42	106.7
3	76	7.6	22	55.9	43	109.2
3½	89	8.9	23	58.4	44	111.8
4	102	10.2	24	61.0	45	114.3
4½	114	11.4	25	63.5	46	116.8
5	127	12.7	26	66.0	47	119.4
6	152	15.2	27	68.6	48	121.9
7	178	17.8	28	71.1	49	124.5
8	203	20.3	29	73.7	50	127.0

YARDS TO METRES

YARDS	METRES	YARDS	METRES	YARDS	METRES	YARDS	METRES	YARDS	METRES
⅛	0.11	2⅛	1.94	4⅛	3.77	6⅛	5.60	8⅛	7.43
¼	0.23	2¼	2.06	4¼	3.89	6¼	5.72	8¼	7.54
⅜	0.34	2⅜	2.17	4⅜	4.00	6⅜	5.83	8⅜	7.66
½	0.46	2½	2.29	4½	4.11	6½	5.94	8½	7.77
⅝	0.57	2⅝	2.40	4⅝	4.23	6⅝	6.06	8⅝	7.89
¾	0.69	2¾	2.51	4¾	4.34	6¾	6.17	8¾	8.00
⅞	0.80	2⅞	2.63	4⅞	4.46	6⅞	6.29	8⅞	8.12
1	0.91	3	2.74	5	4.57	7	6.40	9	8.23
1⅛	1.03	3⅛	2.86	5⅛	4.69	7⅛	6.52	9⅛	8.34
1¼	1.14	3¼	2.97	5¼	4.80	7¼	6.63	9¼	8.46
1⅜	1.26	3⅜	3.09	5⅜	4.91	7⅜	6.74	9⅜	8.57
1½	1.37	3½	3.20	5½	5.03	7½	6.86	9½	8.69
1⅝	1.49	3⅝	3.31	5⅝	5.14	7⅝	6.97	9⅝	8.80
1¾	1.60	3¾	3.43	5¾	5.26	7¾	7.09	9¾	8.92
1⅞	1.71	3⅞	3.54	5⅞	5.37	7⅞	7.20	9⅞	9.03
2	1.83	4	3.66	6	5.49	8	7.32	10	9.14

Index